# As If Art Matters

Modern and post modern art

Reviews and commentary

By

Alec Clayton

Cover art: "Spinner," acrylic painting by Thornton Willis
Cover design by Alec and Gabi Clayton

Dedicated to Debbi Lester, publisher of Art Access, and Ron Swarner, my editor at The Weekly Volcano.

Thanks to Ron Hinson, artist and teacher, who read every word more than once and helped me to more clearly state my case. Ron and I have spent many hours discussing art over the past twenty years, and I have learned a lot from our discussions.

Second edition - expanded


ISBN 978-0-9800322-4-6
printed in the USA

Also by Alec Clayton

Fiction
**Until the Dawn**
**Imprudent Zeal**
**The Wives of Marty Winters**

Books by Alec Clayton available online at

www.alecclayton.com
www.claytonworks.com/publishing/
www.amazon.com

ClaytonWorks Publishing

# Table of Contents



**Reviews**

# Introduction

Art has been a part of my life for as long as I can remember. My mother was a painter. She began studying painting when I was a small child. She called herself a Sunday painter. For someone with practically no training and very little experience, she was damn good, and she instilled in me a lasting love of art. She set up an easel for me right next to hers. I did my first oil painting, a still life with apples and oranges, when I was six years old.

There were art books in the house that I constantly pored over. I devoured pictures of Michelangelo's Sistine ceiling and Renoir's luscious ladies and Picasso's strange blue and rose period paintings. The print quality in those reproductions was probably terrible, but I had no way of judging that back when I was seven or eight years old. And I had no criteria by which to judge what was good or bad art. I loved van Gogh and Michelangelo and El Greco and Peter Paul Rubens (not so much Rubens anymore), but I wasn't very much impressed with Leonardo da Vinci and didn't much care for Cézanne I remember reading about how Cezanne saw objects as simple geometric forms. That was cool to read about, but it didn't necessarily make me like his pictures. But gradually over the years I began to appreciate his art. I think I was also intimidated by Cezanne. I thought that if educated people who knew a lot about art thought he was great and I could not see what was so great about his art, then maybe something was lacking in my education or in my taste. I was reminded of that years later when I was leading a class on a gallery tour and students said they were intimidated by museums and galleries. Perhaps part of my reason for writing about art is to help people learn to view art with a critical and discerning eye without being intimidated.

My mother and her art books were my first teachers. I would try to mimic the style of great artists, often with absurd results. As a typical example of how bumbling my efforts were, I tried to paint in the style of Jackson Pollock using a brush and painting on an easel, not knowing that Pollock poured and dripped the paint onto the canvas. The results were terribly messy and as ugly as homemade sin.

Throughout high school and my first few years as a college art student, my studies were all about learning technique. It wasn't until I met the painter Thornton Willis that I began to realize there was more to art than technique. Thornton was a senior and I was a freshman; he apparently saw some hope in my bumbling efforts and encouraged me. A few years later — after he had gone to graduate school and come back as a new teacher, and after I had dropped out of school and then returned — Thornton and I shared a studio, and he introduced me to ideas and to artists I'd never before been aware of. Suddenly there was much more to art than simply being able to draw a tree that looked like a tree. I realized what I had probably sensed way back when I started painting in my mother's studio: that art was a way to express deeply felt emotions or to question and comment upon the world in which we live. And I began to realize that if I was going to spend my life making pictures, I damn well better start to figure out what makes a picture good. What's the difference between good art and bad art? Or is there such as thing as good and bad art?

So I studied and studied, and by the time I finished graduate school, I thought I pretty much had all the answers. My arrogance knew no bounds.

By the time I started writing art criticism in the mid-eighties, my youthful arrogance had abated somewhat. But I still thought I was pretty hot stuff. I was like Bill Nye the "Science Guy" on TV who boasted, "I know more than you do because I've got a master's degree — in science."

In addition to writing about art, I was teaching in a university art department at the time. That's when my education really began. I learned much more from teaching than I had ever learned as a student. I also learned a lot from fellow teachers Harry Ward and Jim Meade. And since that time I have learned even more from writing about art. I have discovered that when I sit down and try to write about a work of art I began to see things in it that I didn't see when looking at it in the gallery.

It's a cliché, I know, but it's true: the more I learn about art, the less I understand it. But as a painter and a critic, and forever a student, I feel compelled to share my thoughts with others.

I write art criticism as a way of promoting visual art. It gives me pleasure to be able to tell the public about area art exhibits and encourage them to see for themselves. I also hope that my writing will encourage the viewer to look at art with a more critical eye. It especially pleases me when someone tells me a review of mine helped them "get it." That's really what this is all about.

The first section of this book consists of commentary that I have written in an attempt to come to grips with certain ideas.

The second section consists of reviews, with national and international artists first, followed by regional artists in the Pacific Northwest. All of the shows reviewed were in Seattle, Tacoma and Olympia, Washington. I have edited and re-written many of the reviews since the originally appeared in print, either to improve syntax or to eliminate outdated material. In some cases I have combined reviews written for different publications or reviews of different exhibitions by the same artists over time, in which case I have edited them to avoid unnecessary repetition.

## The case against wall fodder

The critic Clement Greenberg was famous for visiting artists' studios, looking at works in progress and pronouncing, "That's a painting" or "That's not a painting" — not this is a good painting, or even this painting has promise but needs a little work, but simply it is or is not a painting. OK, he was not always that cold. Often he would make specific suggestions, and these suggestions were much appreciated by at least some of the artists. But his reputation was based on his more autocratic statements, thus the nickname "Pope Clement."[1]

As a self-critical painter, I feel almost compelled to make equally harsh judgments, or at the very least to constantly question what is or is not art. (My wife jokingly calls me an art snob.) To compromise, qualify or equivocate would be to settle for mediocrity. But as a critic whose job it is to pass judgment on the work of others, I can't bring myself to be that harsh. I know how much work it takes for an artist to put together a show, and I am well aware of what courage it takes to put the work out there for the public to gawk at. I don't want to belittle or insult the artist with my critical commentary. I want to be encouraging rather than discouraging. So my tendency is to try to find something good to say, even when I do not particularly like the work. On the other hand, I shudder at the prospect that my words could promote acceptance of mediocrity. There is far too much work out there in the world that is trite, banal and uninspired, and I do not want to be responsible for promoting more of the same.

That same tiny voice that whispers in my ear telling me to find good things to say also tells me there's really nothing wrong with a pretty picture of flowers in a vase, even if it's been done a thousand times before and even if this particular picture adds nothing to the experience of art. At least, that voice whispers, it would look nice over someone's couch. The colors are pleasing, and you have to give the artist credit for being able to blend brush stokes so smoothly. But another voice tells me that this picture is the visual equivalent of a sappy romance novel. That voice asks me how I could possibly live with myself if I encouraged people to go see and — heaven help us — even buy such tripe. This voice tells me that dignifying such work as art belittles the lifelong struggles of the people who create real art.

At this point it may be necessary to explain what I mean by real art. I use the term "real" to imply quality, and something beyond quality that may be indefinable. If I were writing in a more casual style I might say something like "the real deal" or "the real McCoy," and I imagine everyone would "get my drift." Real in this sense implies something more basic than good or bad. It means true, not fake, not pretentious, like real hardwood floors instead of laminate; gourmet food instead of processed TV dinners, truly felt emotion as opposed to crocodile tears. If I were to use the worst sort of analogy imaginable, I'd refer to the definition of pornography: I may not know what it is, but I know it when I see it. But I have to be careful when I talk about that indefinable something called quality. For a long time during the mid-twentieth century artists were accepted or rejected from museum and gallery exhibitions of the basis of undefined quality, until feminist artists began to point out that it was always women and minorities who were rejected.

But I am straying from the subject.

To my way of thinking, art should at least aspire toward the real in the sense of being not-fake, not-pretentious. It should aspire toward the transformative or transcendental, a tall order, I know.

The artists of the Italian Renaissance saw themselves as godlike or as God's messengers on earth. Few artists today have such lofty ideas, but if there is a secular equivalent of that Renaissance ideal, then that is what artists should aspire toward. To follow through on the religious analogy, I'm reminded of the old saying: If your reach does not exceed your grasp, then what is heaven for?

Real art offers a maximum of variety and excitement within a unified whole. It evokes a deep emotional response. It questions, challenges, provokes and often upsets. It looks at the world in new or unique ways and often forces the viewer to re-evaluate previously held beliefs. It is seldom safe or easy, and although it may be beautiful in a profound way, it is hardly ever pretty. Everything else — the vast majority of so-called art that I like to call wall fodder — falls short of being real art. Wall fodder may be pretty, decorative, cute or enjoyable, but it is not art.[2]

The specific qualities that differentiate art from wall fodder are so numerous and varied that the subject has been touched upon in hundreds of books and hashed out in thousands of seminars and discussion groups. It would be terribly presumptuous of me to say what is and what is not art, but by posing the question I can at least hope to stimulate people to develop the critical discernment necessary for a more fully aware appreciation of art.[3]

And I can suggest that the most important tool in developing that level of discernment is simply to look. Look often and look long.

If you stand in a gallery and watch the other patrons, you will notice that most of them will spend about five seconds with each work of art. But every once in a while you'll notice someone spending long minutes with each painting. You'll notice that he or she backs away to look at it from a distance, and then moves in extremely close to examine it almost as if with a magnifying glass. This viewer will wander around looking at other works, but then return over and over again to the same one or two works. That person is really looking. Chances are that person is another artist. That person might even be me.

## In the caldron

What you have just read is the text of a talk I gave at a discussion group. After I reached my cute little end statement: "That person might even be me," I was met with dead stares from the group. Perhaps I had misjudged my audience.

I encouraged them to comment or ask questions. The first question came from a woman who wanted to know if Tiffany was an artist or a craftsman. My first thought was: Tiffany? Isn't she a pop singer? Oh no, I think she means the guy who made all those glass lampshades. "A crafts person," I answered, and tried — rather unsuccessfully, I fear — to explain my reasoning.

Then there was a fellow who said, "I consider myself an artist. I tie flies."

I don't remember what I said, but I remember thinking: You may fool the fish, buddy, but you don't fool me.

One lady told me she had seen some Picasso paintings once, and they were all full of ugly angles. And the Tiffany lady said, "Surely you don't think Andy Warhol is an artist." I politely informed her that I wouldn't touch that with a ten-foot pole (especially not with that group), and then I exited — as gracefully as possible — thinking: These are the folks for whom wall fodder was invented.

Ah, but that's so smug of me. It's taking the easy way out. If art matters, and it does matter very much, then those of us who write about art should feel compelled to make it as clear as possible. And I do feel so compelled. That's why I'm writing these words. What I would love to do is say in clear and simple words: There is a lot of junk out there that masquerades as art, and if you cannot see the difference between wall fodder and the real thing you are missing out on something that will greatly enhance your experience of life. Following that, I would like to be able to say: This is the way you tell the difference. I would like to be able to list the necessary ingredients that make good art good. If there were such a recipe, we could all go into galleries with checklist in hand and check off a dash of balance and a measure of contrast and three parts texture — and then know whether or not we are looking at good art. Of course, there is no such recipe, and if there were, the first item on the list would probably be: Art does not adhere to recipes.

The best I can do is suggest some things to look for. Please understand that these are merely guiding principles, and that for each principle there are countless exceptions.

## The technique trap

I know what it takes to paint an apple that looks so succulent you want to bite right into the canvas or to paint a figure that looks like a sharp-focus photograph. My mother was able to capture the look and feel of an orange on a table or a river at sunset with a kind of impressionistic truthfulness that was amazing, and she did it after only a few lessons and a year or so painting. I tried to develop an equal facility through six years of college and countless years drawing and painting. I was never able to match her skill. Some people must be born with it, and if they're not, it must take heroic efforts to develop it. So, I can definitely admire technical skill in the visual arts. But I also know that technical facility can hide shortcomings such as an utter lack of idea, conviction or passion. And I'm convinced that when viewers are seduced by amazing technique, they may not see past the flash and polish to discover that there is really nothing there.

I've developed a kind of radar that warns me away from slick art. If the surface is highly polished and the frame looks more elaborate than the painting, my first reaction is to back off and start questioning: What's really here? Is the obvious technical skill a means to an end or is it an end in itself? If there is narrative content, does it ask probing questions or stimulate thought, or if it is purely decorative is it unique and interesting? Are there stimulating contrasts of visual elements and does everything seem to fit together?

No matter what the subject or "message" of a painting, a painting is nothing more or less than an arrangement of shapes on a flat surface. These shapes can look like imaginary or real objects in the world, or they can be shapes that have no relationship to anything outside of the work. How well these objects are painted certainly matters, but what matters more is why they are there and how they are arranged in relation to one another. If they depict something real or imagined, they should tell a meaningful story or trigger an emotional response, and if they do not refer to anything beyond the canvas, they should at the very least be interesting shapes or colors that fit together in some kind of visual design. Virtuosity is not art. Beware the slick surface that covers a vacuous heart.

## Variety within unity

Variety within unity is pretty much a necessity in any art, whether it be painting or literature or music. Literature provides variety through various characters, each with his or her personal idiosyncrasies, through a variety of sentence structures, and by introducing the inevitable conflict or contrast. And it provides unity through the author's voice, through the logical arrangement of chapters, through consistency of character (hopefully with a surprise or two thrown in), and through such devices as repeating similar images or metaphors. Music provides variety by changing accents and volumes and by the use of a multitude of sounds, and it unifies through harmony and rhythm.

The visual arts, of course, do all of the same things. Variety in the visual arts comes through contrasts of shapes and colors, and through an infinite diversity in the quality and types of lines and other marks. And there are countless ways to unify these various visual elements. Cézanne, for instance, used the same choppy brushstroke throughout his pictures, and he would always have an arm or a tree or some other object parallel to the edge of the canvas, which emphasized the flat, rectangular format and created a kind of frame within the frame that held everything together. Picasso unified his pictures through the use of linear design, with lines that would enclose shapes in one area and leave them open in others. In many of his pictures the same contour line would define more than one shape, thus locking it all together like pieces in a jigsaw puzzle. Other devices used to unify various elements are repetition of shapes or colors, or keeping everything keyed to a limited value range (as in music: singing in key). No matter the contrivances used to bring the pieces together, in the best works everything seems to fit.

## The signature of the artist

In the works of most famous or respected artists there can be found what is commonly thought of as their signature look or style. Or perhaps it is more than a look. Perhaps it is content or subject matter that is recognizable as being typical of a particular artist. When I speak of the signature of the artist I am not referring to the artist's name affixed to a work of art. I'm speaking of his or her identity as recognizable due to certain typical elements, which can be related to content or form or some combination of form and content. Turbulent seas and blazing sunsets, for instance, constitute a J.M.W. Turner signature; lonely people in bleak urban scenes an Edward Hopper signature; and interlaced webs of black, white and silver lines are a Jackson Pollock signature. Common or banal imagery painted with oversized comic book-style dot patterns are a Roy Lichtenstein signature.

Despite a wide range of styles within his body of work, a Picasso is almost universally recognized as a Picasso — an obvious exception being works done in the early years of Cubism when paintings by Picasso and Braque were so much alike that hardly anyone could recognize which were done by which artist. Pollock's drip paintings are virtually unmistakable to anyone familiar with his work; and even though his painting style, in theory, should be easy to emulate, few artists have ever attempted to do so and even fewer have done so successfully.

Possible examples are infinite.

The presence of a signature in the sense of an unmistakable look may not be a necessary element of good art, but it may be a good barometer, because a signature look is something that develops naturally as a byproduct of years of study and practice. Good artists do not become good overnight. They develop their skills and expand upon their inherent talents after years of hard work, and in many cases their signatures become increasingly recognizable as they mature.

A signature look, however, should not be confused with a gimmick or hook — the artistic equivalent of a comedian's shtick, such as Henny Youngman's one-liners of Tommy Smothers' "Mom liked you best." Typical examples of gimmicks that are sometimes confused with a signature look can be found in the works of hack artists such as Bev Doolittle and Thomas Kinkade. Both turn out artworks almost as if on an assembly line and both are very popular and financially successful. Doolittle uses variations of the same trick in almost every painting. Her basic trick is to put a spotted pony in a dappled grove of trees; i.e., camouflage. It's a neat trick, but she's repeated it about a million times, and it gets boring quickly. Kinkade turns out factory reproductions of paintings that look like 1920s greeting cards. His "paintings" are actually photographic reproductions upon which he paints a dab or two by hand in order to give them a personal touch.

Recognizing such charlatans is simply a matter of looking. It always comes down to looking: look often and look long. Keep looking, and as you look you will notice that the wall fodder starts to get really, really boring, while the good stuff gets better and better.

I mention this because I am writing for a general audience that I imagine includes a number of beginning art collectors. I would warn beginning collectors to beware of eye-catching gimmicks that may quickly lose their appeal. Revisit a work often and over time if possible.

## The integrity of the picture plane

In the 1950s and '60s, when my generation came of age, World Art was synonymous with Western Art — and almost exclusively American Art, which grew out of Western European traditions. I mention this because the subject of this section, the integrity of the picture plane, is a Western Art concept.

From about 1955 to 1975, give or take a few years, one of the most oft-repeated catch phrases in the world of art was "the integrity of the picture plane." To oversimplify a complicated theory, maintaining the integrity of the picture plane means recognizing that a painting is an arrangement of colors on a flat surface. During the Renaissance, painting was thought to be a window on the world, and this window looked out on a world of linear perspective. Artists created illusions of deep, three-dimensional space on a two-dimensional surface. But even then, the best artists limited their illusions of space in order to make everything fit together in a two-dimensional design. (Incidentally, people now look at Renaissance paintings and marvel at how real they look in comparison to modern art. This illusion of reality is due in large part to the use of perspective and the smooth blending of brush strokes. But if these people who hold the old masters up as an example of real art would take the effort to really look, they would see that the best of today's photo-realist paintings look more real than the best of old master paintings.)[4]

Beginning with Edouard Manet in the mid-1800s, an awareness of the flat surface of the canvas became increasingly important. The Impressionists' use of high-value colors laid side by side with little blending or modeling brought everything closer to the surface. Later, the Cubists did away with linear perspective. Flatness became a hallmark of the abstract artists of the early to mid-twentieth century. Critics such as Clement Greenberg, the leading champion of Abstract Expressionism, lauded flatness. Teachers in art departments across the land began preaching flatness to their students. The idea was to recognize and celebrate the reality of painting, which was that a painting was an arrangement of shapes on a flat surface. Nothing more and nothing less. Anything that detracted from this, including perspective and recognizable subject matter, detracted from the art. Any illusion and any reference to things outside of the painting itself was taboo. Inherent in this way of thinking was the concept that art was defined narrowly as painting. Sculpture, pottery, photography and other visual art forms were considered less important than painting. Of course, as I indicated earlier, this is an over simplification; it is a description of a concept at its most extreme. Yet many an artist, critic and teacher took it to that extreme.

Paintings became flatter and flatter and flatter until finally, sometime in the 1970s, people began to rebel against flatness, and illusory space once again began to appear. (As a by-product of this rediscovery of space, many lesser-known Renaissance artists were rediscovered and became role models for post-modernist artists.)

In many ways I believe the re-introduction of illusory space in painting is a good thing because it has expanded possibilities. But, on the other hand, I think throwing flatness out the window is throwing the baby out with the bathwater. I may be willing to allow a certain amount of illusory space to creep back into painting, but I think an awareness of the integrity of the picture plane is still a good indicator that the artist is more than a little bit sophisticated. It indicates, at the very least, an awareness of visual dynamics — that, for example, every overlapping mark and every contrasting juxtaposition of soft and hard edges create illusions of space and that color contrasts may be more vibrant when patches of color rest on the same plane. Such an awareness of visual dynamics may be a good argument for keeping modern paintings flat, or at the very least limiting depth to a succession of overlapping picture planes. (I know that some post-modernists would say I'm being regressive, and they may be right, but at the very least I believe contemporary artists have to be aware of all the spatial implications of their work.)

## The message vs. the look

During the same time period when "the integrity of the picture plane" was the catch phrase of the day, there was a belief that how a picture was painted was more important than what the picture depicted. The way it looked was more important than what it represented. Sculptures were no longer depictions of heroes on horseback, but became burnished metal surfaces arranged in space; paintings were no longer pictures of flowers and trees and beautiful women, but were all about the contrast and harmony of shapes and colors. The formal aspects of art became more important than the message or subject matter.

But the same people who rebelled against flatness also rebelled against the primacy of form, and the pendulum swung toward primacy of content. It doesn't matter, these champions of content said, if a picture is badly painted; it doesn't matter if the colors are ugly and the shapes are uninventive and the drawing is crude; what matters is the message the art conveys.[5]

Perhaps this gives away my prejudices (not to mention my age), but I believe visual art has to be visually exciting. No matter how profound the message may be, if it is not presented in a visually exciting way, then it is literature or theater or something else, but it is not visual art. Despite some contemporary theories that say the purposes of art are more political, social or ecological than aesthetic, I believe a strong aesthetic element is still necessary. I still believe a work of visual art should be a transformative work of aesthetic beauty.

This would seem to cast aside many contemporary forms such as video and multi-media installations and performance art, but I believe these new art forms need to be judged by different criteria, or perhaps new forms create a need for newer ideas about what constitutes beauty.

Art that is presented as visual, no matter how conceptual, must be judged formally as well as conceptually, and that means taking into consideration such things as the balance and harmony of color and line. Even if I were to concede that there are cases in which content can take precedence over form, then the message had better be pretty damn profound. If the message is simply that ripe apples on a blue cloth are pretty, or that racial discrimination is not a good thing, or that politicians can be corrupt, that's stating the obvious and that's not enough. To be considered good art, the message has to be not only original or profound, it has to be stated in a unique or compelling or visually exciting way.

## The case for originality

That original art should be original is almost too obvious for words, but many paintings seen in galleries are not original. To me, the word "original" means more than simply something that is not a reproduction; it means more than that the artist did it all by herself with her own two hands; it means something that has never before been done in quite the same way. The most common of all examples of what I call wall fodder is painting in the style of the French Impressionists. The world is flooded with watered-down versions of landscapes by Monet and Renoir. Monet and Renoir created beautiful art, but they did it well over a century ago. We've seen quite enough, and their followers are seldom half as good as them anyway, so what's the point?

This brings up two questions. The first is: Is truly original art even possible considering how much has already been done? And the second is: Say artist X paints water lilies in a pond in the style of Monet, and he does it just as well as Monet did it (highly unlikely, but this is hypothetical), then wouldn't that be good art even if it were not original?

My answer to the first question is yes, it is still possible to be original, but it may be a question of just how original is original. The first person to ever use perspective in a drawing was truly original. Picasso and Braque were certainly original when they invented Cubism. Nothing like that had ever been done before. But they based their work on things that had previously been hinted at by Cézanne, and as everybody knows, Picasso borrowed ideas from everyone and everything. Still, he put his borrowed ideas to use in unique ways. When Jackson Pollock started painting on the floor instead of the easel and dripped his paint from sticks onto his canvas instead of painting with a brush, and created all-over patterns with no beginning or end (as opposed to the tradition of painting shapes onto a background) — when he did all of this, he was not doing anything that had not been done before. Plenty of other artists had already dripped paint, and Mark Toby was already painting all-over patterns, but nobody had ever before done all of these things together the way he did, and so Pollock's drip paintings were truly original. The point is, while being absolutely original may be next to impossible, being relatively original is not only possible, it is necessary. If you can't do something that has never before been done, then at least do something in a new way.

My answer to the question about artist X painting water lilies just like Monet is that no matter how beautiful it may be, it's not art. Let's put it this way: If I really put my mind to it I could probably write my own version of "Romeo and Juliet," and it might be just as good as the one Shakespeare wrote, but nobody would consider me a literary genius for having done it. On the other hand, when Arthur Laurents rewrote "Romeo and Juliet" as a contemporary love story set to music and called it "West Side Story," that was pretty damn original.

While familiarity may have an attraction all its own, we all know what familiarity breeds. If we've seen sunsets in nature that are strikingly beautiful, then when we see a painting of a sunset we are apt to be attracted to it precisely because it reminds us of something we have already seen and grown to love. Not because it is art. I would rather go outside and look at the real thing.

## Familiarity breeds contempt

I've noticed an interesting phenomenon. When I go into an art gallery I may immediately spot a work of art that I like, and perhaps another one that I don't like so much. But after spending some time in the gallery, I begin to notice that the one I liked doesn't look quite as good as I had at first thought, and the one I didn't like gradually begins to look better and better. It's amazing how often this happens.

I think this happens because, in the case of the work we initially like but soon grow tired of, we are attracted to the familiar. The familiar is comfortable; we're predisposed to like it. That's why people go to see "The Nutcracker" every year at Christmas, and then go home and watch "It's a Wonderful Life" on television for the umpteenth time. But the familiarity that attracts us soon wears thin. It may be that the painting we did not like at first put us off because of its originality, because it does not offer the comfort of familiarity.

Mediocre art gives easy pleasure. Like ice cream, it is sweet and goes down easy, but its pleasure is not long lasting. It is nothing more than wall fodder. Art that is worthy of being called art, on the other hand, is seldom easy to digest but always worth the effort.

1 - My quote of Clement Greenberg may have been misleading. When he pronounced a work of art either a painting or not a painting, he was being purposefully dramatic. Reading Greenberg's reviews makes it abundantly clear that he recognized an infinite range of grays between the black hole of non-painting and the clear white light of painting. Similarly, I know there are many shades of gray between real art and wall fodder. But I too like to be dramatic at times.

2 - The term "wall fodder." comes from Willie Ray Parish, a sculptor in El Paso, Texas. His wife, Becky Hendrick (a fine painter and art critic) informed me that he got it from her and that she got it from an LA Weekly article by Peter Plagens.

3 - When I use the term "art" in this context, I am thinking primarily of painting. There would be more exceptions to my comments if I were to discuss sculpture, environmental art, mixed-media installations, video and performance art and so forth.

4 -Realism in art has two distinct meanings. It can refer to the opposite of idealism, as in gritty, honest and uncompromising, or it can refer to the illusion that the object depicted is a real object in three-dimensional space. In this context, I am referring to illusory realism.

5 -During the '70s, it seemed that the only thing that mattered was the idea. IDEA — all caps and italicized — was king, so much so that Tom Wolfe wrote a deliciously funny (but totally stupid) book about it called *The Painted Word*.

# Abstract Art and Figurative Art

**"The big artist keeps a sharp eye on Nature and steals her tools. ...then he's got a canoe of his own, smaller than Nature's but big enough for every purpose. ...With this canoe he can sail parallel to Nature's sailing." - Thomas Eakins** [1]

**"I am nature." Jackson Pollock** [2]

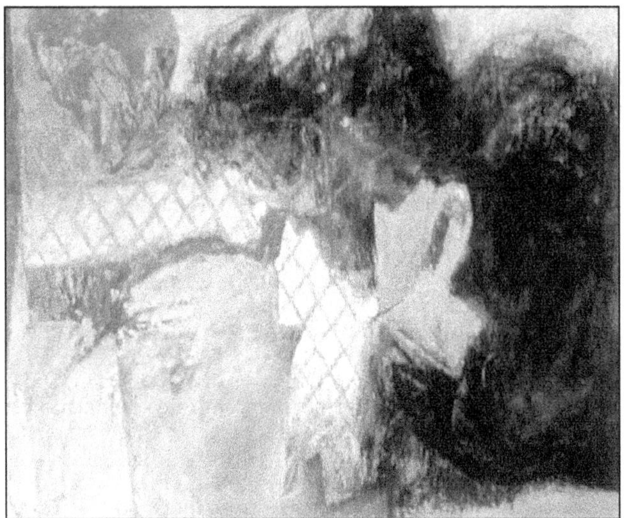

*Alec Clayton, "Cave Dweller" oil on canvas, 51" x 41," 1994*

---

Throughout the twentieth century the big tug-of-war among contemporary artists was between abstract art and figurative art. Many artists vacillated between the two. Leading figurative artists such as Roy Lichtenstein and Phillip Pearlstein started out as abstract painters (and Pearlstein always maintained that even his photo-realistic figures were really abstract paintings). And Richard Diebenkorn, when he was just beginning to become known as a major figure painter, switched to abstraction and became even more famous — while Fairfield Porter and Edward Hopper were unfairly cast in the role of minor painters because they refused to jump on the abstraction bandwagon. Even Willem de Kooning and Jackson Pollock, the leading abstract painters at the time, were accused of betraying the modernist movement when they introduced figurative elements into their work.

Painters came to blows over the war between figuration and abstraction. And many people in the general public were bewildered by abstraction. Statements such as "a six-year-old child could do that" became common, because people could not see in abstraction a way to judge what was good and what wasn't.

Abstract art first reared its head at the beginning of the twentieth century, and even at the end of the century many people were still bewildered by it. In 1999, I was invited to do a show at the Henderson House Museum in Tumwater, Washington. The museum director asked me if I would write a brief statement on my paintings that would offer guidance to people who were not familiar with abstract art.

Before presenting that statement, it might be helpful if I explain that the commonly held meaning of the term *abstract* has changed over time. At one time to abstract meant to draw from or summarize. Abstract art was not necessarily without recognizable subject matter, but it might distort, simplify or *abstract* an object's appearance, perhaps to express an emotional reaction or bring out the essence or core of the subject.

Art with no recognizable subject matter was once called nonobjective or nonrepresentational art, but through common usage abstract art has come to mean what was once meant by nonobjective, and it is in the broader sense that I use the term here — meaning essentially (but not strictly) nonobjective.

## Abstract Art:<br>an essay written for the Henderson House Museum

Wassily Kandinsky is generally credited with making the first abstract paintings at the beginning of the twentieth century. Kandinsky spoke of his paintings as being symbolic and as relating to music: symbolic in that colors and shapes have inherent associations (red associated with fire, passion, etc.; blue associated with cool water and summer skies) and musical in the use of rhythm, harmony and accent.

The problem with "understanding" such art often comes from the very attempt to understand. People faced with abstract art are often put off because they fear if they can't understand what it means they will appear dumb. But interesting shapes and beautiful colors can be enjoyed for what they are in and of themselves without having to puzzle out what they might mean. We all have the ability to look at the soft dreaminess of cloud patterns and be swept up by their beauty. We all have the ability to appreciate the brilliant colors and intricate markings in a flower without having to ask what the flower means. We should be able to do the same with abstract paintings, without believing we have to understand the deeper underlying meaning — often there is none.

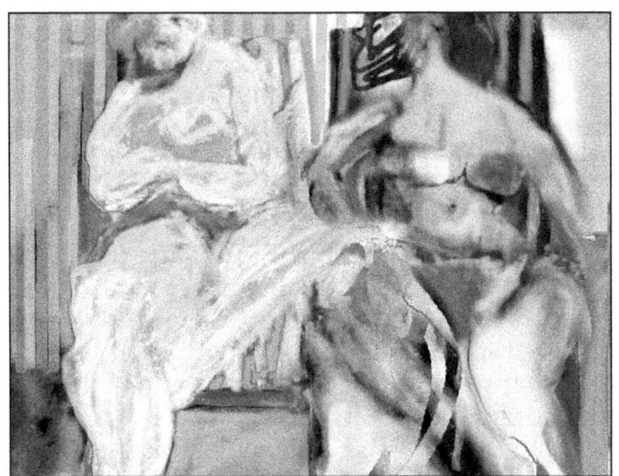

*Alec Clayton, "Green With Envy," computer art, various dimensions, 2006*

---

Kandinsky's reference to music is helpful. A song with lyrics may tell a story or express emotions with which we can easily relate. But beyond the lyrics, we can feel the emotions and enjoy the abstract elements of music: rhythm, harmony, the unexpected accent that delights, the range of a singer's voice, the power of the drummer's beat. By way of analogy, instrumental music is like abstract art. In art we can "listen" to the rhythms of repetitive shapes. We can "hear" the harmony of blended colors and feel the power of a deep red next to a velvety black. An abstract painting is visual music without lyrics.

My paintings are informed by nature. If you study them carefully you will see fish and birds and flowers and human figures, but these figures are never obvious. I don't want to paint a bird that looks like a bird, because then the viewer will be looking at the bird instead of the paint. Finding the bird or the face can be fun — like searching for Waldo — but the images are not what the paintings are about. What the paintings are about is rhythm, texture, contrast and harmony, color, shape and pattern. These are the things viewers should look for in order to get the most out of them. Look to see how this line over here leads the eye to that shape over there, how a pattern on one side is repeated with slight variations on the other side, how a dull color in one place makes the brighter color next to it look even brighter, how contrasting elements are kept from clashing due to the way they seem to weave in and out in space and fit together like pieces of a puzzle.

Ultimately, my paintings are about resolving conflicts ... just like a story, but the "characters" are color, line, shape, etc.

When reviewing art that is abstract but with references to nature, I have observed an interesting phenomenon: the more abstract it is, the better it tends to be. A painter may base her painting on recognizable subject matter, for example, but if she gets too caught up with the challenge of making a bird look like a bird, she loses her spontaneity and loses sight of the overall composition. It is as if subject matter has a natural capacity to corrupt form. But the problem may not be with the subject matter. It may simply be that an artist must not lose sight of what the work is about whether it is abstract or figurative or something in between.

1 - Quoted by Robert Hughes in *Nothing if Not Critical.*
2 - Pollock's reply to Hans Hoffman when Hoffman said he needed the inspiration of nature.

# As If Art Matters

**"...in the greatest painting, the painter communes with himself."**
**- Robert Motherwell [8]**

**"...is a truck in a music school more musical than a truck passing by in the street?"**
**- John Cage [9]**

**"I think it would be so great if more people took up silk screens so that no one would know whether my picture was mine or somebody else's." - Any Warhol [10]**

**"Art is anything you can get away with." Marshall McLuhan [11]**

Those quotes thrilled my little anarchistic heart when I used them in my graduate thesis back in 1970. The thesis argued that the whole juggernaut of art history had come to a screeching halt, and that a new day had arrived in which everything was art and all barriers between art and life had vanished.

In typical graduate thesis style, my thesis had a rather high and mighty title. It was: *A Ground for Today's Art: An Alternative to the Frame-Pedestal Aesthetic.* Looking back, I'm pretty proud of that work because in it I clearly laid down ideas that were just beginning to percolate among artists and critics in the world art capitals. I was more ahead of my time than I realized, although I have tempered and/or rejected some of the ideas I championed back then.[12]

A new thought took hold of the collective art mind in the late 1960s and early 1970s. The thought was: *Why not?* Or, to put it another way: *Says who?* In the previous decades, Abstract-Expressionist painting so dominated the world art that it seemed to be the only art worthy of the name. But it was a time when everyone was questioning authority, and none more so than artists. So they questioned everything: Why can't pieces of felt material scattered on the floor be art? Why not paint pictures in the style of medieval illustrated manuscripts or Renaissance frescoes? Who says a painting can't have figures or three-point perspective and tell stories, or make jokes or belittle the sacred cows of art and politics?

Who says that painting and sculpture are the only viable visual arts? Why not incorporate sound and movement into a work of art? Who, other than the artist, is to say what is or is not art? If I as an artist choose it or think it or do it, who is to say it's not art?

The new thought was spurred by people like Jasper Johns, Robert Rauschenberg, Claes Oldenburg, Andy Warhol and Allan Kaprow; but the initial defining moment that set the stage for the new art probably came about as early as 1917 when Marcel Duchamp bought a urinal from a plumbing supply store, titled it "Fountain" and entered it in an art exhibition under the pseudonym R. Mutt (actually the name of a manufacturer of sanitary hardware). The piece was rejected from the exhibition. Duchamp wrote a letter objecting to the rejection:

> They say any artist paying six dollars may exhibit. Mr. Mutt sent in a fountain. Without discussion this article disappeared and never was exhibited.
>
> What were the grounds for refusing Mr. Mutt's fountain:
>
> 1. Some contend it was immoral, vulgar.
> 2. Others, it was plagiarism, a plain piece of plumbing.
>
> Now Mr. Mutt's fountain is not immoral, that is absurd, no more than a bathtub is immoral. It is a fixture that you see every day in plumbers' show windows. Whether Mr. Mutt with his own hands made the fountain or not has no importance. He CHOSE it, he took an ordinary article of life, placed it so that its significance disappeared under the new title and point of view — created a new thought for that object.
>
> As for plumbing, that is absurd. The only works of art America has given are her plumbing and her bridges. [13]

Beginning in the '60s and continuing right on through the end of the century, the why not/says who attitude spawned countless movements, from Pop and Op to happenings and environments and performance art, to Neo this and Neo that, to all kinds of combinations and assimilations of everything that ever has been. Everything was lumped together under the rubric *Post-modernism*, and somewhere along the way someone came up with the word *pluralism*, which has become the guiding principle or everything post-modern. All styles, fashions, ideas are worthy. Everything goes.

So what's the latest trend? Everything.

One of the good things about the post-modern zeitgeist is that a lot of good art that had been overlooked in the past has resurfaced, and great artists of the past who had been out of favor have been rediscovered. Women and minorities who had never before been given the recognition they disserved have come into their own. Art forms such as weaving and quilting and pottery that previously had been shown only in crafts fairs and gift shops began appearing in major museums and galleries (witness the phenomenon of the Gee's Bend quilters). Photography took on a new importance as photographers such as Sandy Skoglund and Cindy Sherman began to do large-scale photographs that rivaled the great paintings of the day. Commercial artists and designers, and even comic book artists, began to gain museum recognition. It was a new day, egalitarian and democratic, and I loved it.

But I began to notice, sometime in the mid-'80s, that there was a downside to all this egalitarianism. Naively, I guess, I had thought the people who took up the challenge laid down by Duchamp and Warhol would be as brilliant as Duchamp and Warhol. Or, at the very least, I thought they would have skills honed by years of art school training and practical experience. I thought that before they banged on their metaphorical pianos with their fists they would have practiced playing scales for years and years — the old saw that you have to master the ground rules before you can break them. And even if the new pluralism opened the doors for just anybody to claim the title *artist*, I thought gallery owners and museum curators and art critics would offer some modicum of quality control. But it turns out that a lot of these folks are mostly influenced by fads and fashion and the bottom line. And those of us who dare to say there should be some qualitative judgment are accused of being elitist.

Quality is an allusive term at best. Who is to say what is good and what is bad? There was a time when you could glance through the art literature and talk to art professionals and see that there was a kind of unspoken consensus among professionals. If most of the professionals agreed that Robert Motherwell and Frank Stella were good artists and Norman Rockwell was a hack, then it was pretty easy to identify quality. Quality art had more in common with Stella than with Rockwell. Again I am over simplifying to illustrate a point.

Feminist artists, however, pointed out the obvious flaws with that line of thinking. The art professionals who were making all the decisions about who got in the shows were all men. White men. And under the guise of quality they were rejecting most works by women and racial minorities.

Quality was hard to define then, and it may be harder now. But it still matters. It matters to the artist, and it matters to the viewer. It matters to the artists because if we do not know where to draw the line, all his or her hard work and study will have been for nothing. It matters to the viewer because less and less quality work is shown in galleries and museums.

When curators and gallery owners base their judgment on what sells and critics base theirs on who is advertising in their publications, and there are no longer any recognized criteria for judging a work of art, everyone is caught in a downward spiral. This downward flow into a cesspool of mediocrity seems an unstoppable juggernaut. Hacks the likes of Robert Kinkade turn out factory-produced paintings of sentimental tripe that sell by the millions, and works by celebrity artists such as David Salle, whose contributions are questionable at best, are purchased by major museums throughout the world, while many more deserving artists get no recognition at all.

Despite it all, serious and unpretentious artists such as Sean Scully and Phillip Pearlstein and Thornton Willis (the latter of whom had his fifteen minutes of fame and then faded in the public eye but still continues to make great paintings) plod along unaffected by fads and trends. Despite it all, art still matters.

8 - Robert Motherwell, "The Modern Painter's World."
9 - John Cage, as quoted by Barbara Rose, *American Art Since 1900.*
10 - Gene Swenson, "What is Pop Art?"
11 - Marshall McLuhan, *The Medium is the Massage.*
12 - Thanks to my thesis advisor Charles Moldovan.
13 - Reprinted from "The Blind Man," 1917, in *The History of Surrealist Painting* by Marcel Jean.

# Reviews

# van Gogh to Mondrian

*Compiled from reviews in Art Access, June 2004, and The Weekly Volcano, June 3, 2004*

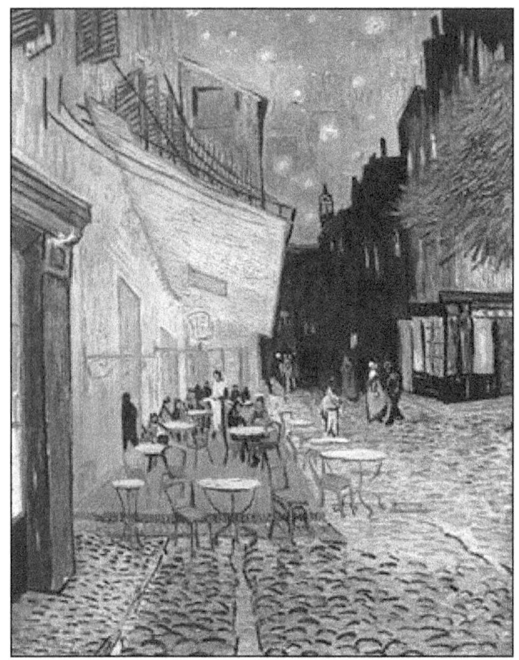

*Vincent van Gogh, "Café Terrace at Night" (Place du Foran), oil on canvas, 31 ¾" x 25 5/8" 1888, courtesy Kroller-Muller Museum, The Netherlands*

"Van Gogh to Mondrian: Modern Art from the Kroller-Muller Museum" at the Seattle Art Museum is an extraordinary exhibition. There are not superlatives enough in the English language to describe it.

The Kroller-Muller's van Gogh collection is the second largest in the world, second only to the van Gogh Museum in Amsterdam, and most of the Dutch master's 12 paintings and 10 drawings from the collection that are included in this show have never been seen in the United States.

Helene Kroller-Muller and her industrialist husband, Anton, began seriously collecting art around 1906. They collected the leading Symbolists, Neo-Impressionist and Cubist painters. Her favorites were van Gogh and Mondrian, both of whom she collected when no one else would buy their works. She was Mondrian's patron throughout his career. As for van Gogh, in her lifetime she amassed 97 of his paintings and 185 of his drawings. By 1935 her collection had grown so large that she had a museum built for it in the Hoge Veluwe National Park in Holland. The museum was finished just before her death in 1938.

Helene Kroller-Muller once remarked that her ambition was to collect works that would "stand the test of time ...because I collect to give to future generations that which I consider the best in life."

Although van Gogh's paintings are widely reproduced, very few of his original paintings have ever been shown in America, and most of the drawings in this exhibition have seldom even been reproduced.

I can't recall ever seeing an original van Gogh drawing, and although I have been lucky enough to see some of his paintings, it has been well over 30 years, and I had forgotten just how brilliant they are. Suffice it to say the difference between seeing these works in reproduction and in the original is like the difference between looking at a dish of water and diving in the ocean.

The things that stand out most are the clarity and brightness of his colors, and how studied and precise both the drawings and paintings are. This latter quality is a real shock to see, because it goes against everything we have been taught to think about van Gogh. We think of him as being expressive, a highly emotive painter. But every stroke of the brush looks as if it were planned and carefully applied. There appears to be no blending or scumbling of the paint strokes, no painting over or correcting, and absolutely no muddying of his colors.

Among the paintings are: "Café Terrace," that marvelous night scene of the yellow café with empty tables under an awning and a brilliant blue starry sky; a tiny self portrait in glowing pink skin tones; the portrait of Joseph Roulin the postman in his uniform with the Japanese-style floral print wallpaper in the background; the portrait of Madame Roulin; a still life with all of his favorite things (pipe, bottle of absinthe, onion, book and letter); a painting of an olive grove and another of pine trees with broken limbs done shortly before his suicide; and the "Good Samaritan" after a Delacroix painting.

There is also a general impression that van Gogh's drawing was somewhat awkward or clumsy, but there is no hint of clumsiness in these drawings. Every mark is sure and confident, and there is a density of fine detail far beyond what appears in the few drawings that have been widely reproduced.

The half-dozen or so Mondrian paintings are interesting as seen in comparison with the van Goghs because the public thinks of Mondrian as being as cool and calculated as Van Gogh is emotionally expressive; yet there is no indication of correcting or adjusting in the van Goghs, and the Mondrians are full of painted-over evidence of correction. He leaves visual clues to the way he worked out his compositions in process.

It is also interesting to compare Mondrian with Bart van der Leck, who is relatively unknown but whose paintings are very much like Mondrian's. Both were supported by Helene Kroller-Muller in their early careers, but she lost faith in them as their works became progressively abstract. She quit patronizing both of them when she thought they had veered from spiritually based painting into pure abstraction. But then she became Mondrian's patron again when she saw that even though his work was becoming more and more abstract there was an underlying spirituality. For reasons that were never explained, however, she never championed van der Leck again, even though he followed a path almost identical to that of Mondrian.

The exhibition also includes two Picasso paintings, an early portrait of a woman and a small pre-Cubist nude done during the period when he was highly influenced by African masks. There is one whole wall of Pointillist landscapes and a striking interior scene of a family gathered at the table by Paul Signac. Also shown are works by Juan Gris, Fernand Leger, Diego Rivera and others.

The exhibition also includes furniture by Hendrick Petrus Berlage, a large stained glass window by van der Leck, and architectural drawings by Berlage and Henri van der Velde.

# Americans in Paris

*Art Access, January 2004*

Avant-garde art as we came to know it in the twentieth century was primarily forged in the caldron that was Paris, France, in the years between the first and second world wars. It was there and then that writers such as Hemmingway and Fitzgerald met painters the likes of Picasso and Matisse in the home of Gertrude Stein, and from such gatherings — but not only from such gatherings —modernism was born.

To lay all of modernism at the doorstep of Paris and in the commingling of disparate styles that proliferated in the years between the wars is, of course, to oversimplify. We know that in the visual arts the foundations of modernism had already been built. Impressionism had opened the way. Post-Impressionism had forged the path. Cubism and Dada had expanded the horizons.

Paris was a magnet that drew the most advanced artists from the rest of the Western world, especially the United States.

American artists went to Paris to learn, often just to soak up the atmosphere. They brought with them a uniquely American ingenuity and practicality, and the mingling of American and Parisian sensibility was an especially heady mix. From this mix flowed the two streams of modernism that determined the direction of avant-garde art throughout the twentieth century. One stream was abstraction growing out of Cubism that sought purity of form; the other was a conceptual stream flowing from Dada that was based on irony and surprise.

A large selection of paintings, prints, photographs and sculptures from this seminal time period in modern art history is displayed in the exhibition "A Transatlantic Avant-Garde: American Artists in Paris, 1918-1939" from the Musée d'Art Américain Giverny in France, which is now showing at the Tacoma Art Museum. TAM is the only West Coast venue for this exhibition and one of only two American museums to host it (the other being the Terra Museum of American Art in Chicago).

Approximately 130 works are included, featuring works by Alexander Calder, Stuart Davis, Charles Demuth, Man Ray, Marcel Duchamp, Fernand Leger and many others. The exhibition focuses on four thematic groupings. "The Purity of the Object" and "The Birth of Geometric Abstraction" are overlapping themes dealing with primarily post-Cubist works. "The Chemists of Mystery" examines Surrealist and Dadaistic trends, and "Portraits of the Avant-Garde" looks at photographs of the era, the majority of which, in this exhibition, were taken by Man Ray.

There are two ways to enter the galleries, but no matter where you enter, the photographs are the first things you see. One wall is filled with portraits of artists and writers such as Gertrude Stein, Meret Oppenheim, Andre Breton, Jean Cocteau, Marcel Duchamp and James Joyce. Another is filled with Man Ray's rayographs, which are abstract designs Ray created by placing found objects on photographic paper and exposing them to light. These, along with Ray's solarized photographs, were among the first pictures ever to lift photography above mere record keeping.

Near the photographic portraits are two little watercolor portraits of Gerald and Sara Murphy by Fernand Leger, which are notable because they are so atypical of Leger. Whereas his paintings are massively architectonic (even the figures are constructed of spheres and cubes and cylinders), these watercolor portraits are atmospheric and light.

Stuart Davis and Charles Demuth fill a large part of the exhibit. Three of Demuth's cityscapes display his penchant for breaking the planes of architectural form into flat designs with overlapping transparencies that unify his complex forms. Davis's city scenes are fascinating in their quirky details and textures, but they are not among his better works. In his essay for the show's catalog, Kenneth E. Silver says that the work Davis did in Paris was retrograde in comparison with work such as his egg beater series and some of the works based on advertising imagery that he had done in New York before going to Paris. But even lesser works by Davis are better than the best works of many another artist.

Shown in proximity to two large Leger paintings are a large painting and a sculpture by John Storrs, a lesser-known Cubist sculptor. His "Gendarme" is a painted limestone figure of a French policeman rendered in chiseled planes of stark black and white. It is so solid as to appear as man-as-building, a feeling that is heightened due to its placement near Leger. The same solidity of form is manifest in Storrs's oil painting "Monologue."

Under represented in art history but well represented here are a group of painters who were known as the Park Avenue Cubists. These include A.E. Gallatin, George L.K. Morris, Suzy Frelinghuysen and Charles G. Shaw.

Isamu Noguchi, who worked in Paris in the studio of Constantin Brancusi, is best known for his biomorphic sculptures, two of which are included. Noguchi is also represented here with a series of two-dimensional prints that play with the positive and negative interplay of flat, black and white shapes and illustrate just how strongly Brancusi influenced him.

Also shown are Duchamp's famous "Boite en Valise," — a kind of mini-retrospective of his entire life's work displayed in a valise — and works by Alexander Calder, Charles Biederman, Patrick Henry Bruce, Berenice Abbott and others. Plus some Joseph Cornell constructions that seem out of place but which were nice to see nevertheless.

"A Transatlantic Avant-Garde: American Artists in Paris, 1918-1939" offers Washingtonians a rare glimpse at some very important art.

# The Great American Thing

*The Weekly Volcano, January 2006*

Do you remember the Tacoma Art Museum's great show "American Artists in Paris, 1918-1939" from the Musée d'Art Américain Giverny in France? Well now TAM is showing what amounts to the sequel, "The Great American Thing: Modern Art and National Identity, 1915-1935." Taken together, these two shows constitute an impressive survey of American art from that period. It's too bad they couldn't have been combined into one large show, but that might be too overwhelming. Good things may be better digested in smaller bites.

"The Great American Thing" is co-curated by TAM curator Patricia McDonnell and Wanda M. Corn of the Figge Art Museum in Davenport, Iowa. (The exhibition is based on Corn's book of the same name.)

All the big names in early American modernism are represented: photographers Walker Evans, Edward Weston, Margaret Bourke-White, Ansel Adams and Alfred Stieglitz; painters Stuart Davis, Charles Demuth, George Groz, Fernand Léger, Georgia O'Keefe, John Marin, Mark Toby, Joseph Stella, Charles Sheeler, Marsden Hartley, Romare Bearden and Arthur Dove — and let's not forget those bad boys of Dada, Man Ray and Marcel Duchamp.

As you may recall, the cover of the Paris show catalogue featured that marvelous Stuart Davis painting, "New York-Paris, No. 1." Well this show has that painting also, plus Davis's "New York-Paris, No. 2" and his iconic precursor to Pop Art, "Odol."

The show includes approximately 130 works of art plus archival materials such as documentary photographs and film clips and other artifacts from the era.

McDonnell is well versed in art history with a particular emphasis on the era covered by this show, and she and Corn did a wonderful job of breaking the show into groupings based on major themes of importance to American artists between the world wars. America was admired for its engineering, its bridges and skyscrapers and plumbing; the spirit of the jazz age and the jazzy impact of commercial advertising epitomized urban America, while openness of the great Western plains along with Native American traditions influenced the spirituality of the age (most notably epitomized by Georgia O'Keefe's escape to New Mexico). All of these themes are highlighted in this exhibition, as are America's proliferation of inventive consumer goods and its rich folk art heritage.

Archibald J. Motley, Jr's "Blues" is one of the more striking paintings in the show. It is a painting of dancers in a jazz club so small and crowded that the band members are practically sitting in the diner's laps. It beautifully captures the feel of a jazz joint and is nicely composed with a trombone slide, a woman's long arm and strategically placed red and blue highlights in a mostly black and brown sea of closely packed bodies.

Charles Demuth's "Paquebot, Paris" is a marvel of clean design and delicate balance, as are his faceted and crisp paintings of industrial buildings.

One of the more pleasant surprises in the show is Charles Sheeler's "Interior." Mostly noted for Cubist-inspired industrial cityscapes, Sheeler's interior view of tables and still life objects as seen from high overhead looks like a precursor for the kind of patterning we see in Philip Pearlstein figure studies. Another surprise is the similarities between Georgia O'Keefe's "Kachina" and Marsden Hartley's "Painting No. 50." Hartley's iconic abstraction combines elements of German military costuming and Native American ceremonial garb, while O'Keefe's painting of a Native kachina doll also reflects folk art influences — both illustrating the range of influences assimilated by artists of the era.

# In the Presence of Greatness
# The New York School

*The Weekly Volcano, July 2004*

I feel an unexpected and strangely reverent quietude as I enter the third floor gallery at the Tacoma Art Museum. The gallery is empty of people. The lighting is muted in order to protect the delicate works on paper, most of which is non-archival. I sense that I am in the presence of greatness. I knew it coming in, but there is an aura about this exhibition that intensifies that feeling. The show is "The New York School: The Politics of Abstraction." Drawn largely from the Washington Art Consortium Collection and TAM's permanent collection, this exhibition features works on paper by Helen Frankenthaler, Adolf Gottlieb, Jasper Johns, Franz Kline, Lee Krasner, Joan Mitchell, Robert Motherwell, Barnett Newman, Jules Olitski, Jackson Pollock and Robert Rauschenberg.

I'm not sure what I was expecting — perhaps lacy skeins of red, black and silver in a Pollock drip painting, perhaps exuberant explosions of color and frantic line work in a Joan Mitchell. What I did not expect was such a small and colorless exhibition. I look around, and I am struck with how muted and contemplative these works are. I marvel that art such as this, which only a short time ago was considered bombastic, expressionistic and revolutionary, now appears almost quaint. I realize how quickly yesterday's avant-garde paintings become relics of history, like dust-covered tomes hidden away in a library.

A museum statement explains the title and the thesis of the show: "The New York School: The Politics of Abstraction will introduce the thesis, most convincingly argued by Professor of Art History at the University of British Columbia, Serge Guilbaut, that the dominance of 'pure' abstraction was part of a complex social dynamic influenced by cold war politics and the emergence of the United States as a political and economic superpower after World War II."

I read a quote from Clement Greenberg that is printed on the wall. It elucidates the same thesis, that art for art's sake was a political statement. And I think, "Yes, this is all true. But don't we all know that by now? And does it really matter?" And I think, "Sure. Why not? But isn't this just a device around which to organize a show?"

What really matters here, it seems to me, are not the ideas New York School artists may have had about the place and function of art in society. What matters is the formal inventiveness of these artists. They are the ones who developed the visual language that every succeeding generation has worked with (or rebelled against). They legitimized art for art's sake. They gave succeeding generations the freedom to present a line as a line and a shape as a shape, and a painting as an arrangement of shapes and colors on a flat canvas that need not aspire to anything more. What we now think of as Greenbergian formalism was born with these artists, matured quickly, and soon became outdated — all in a historical blink of the eye. Maybe, I think, that's why these works now seem quaint. Perhaps that is a good thing. Perhaps it allows us to see these modest works for what they are. And simply enjoy them.

And there is so much in this show to enjoy. These are spiritual works that speak to the viewer who is willing to listen. The teetering balance of boot-like shapes and ovals in Robert Motherwell's "Spanish Elegy II," for instance, is a marvel that reveals itself only upon long contemplation. Likewise, the way a scruffy circle makes the white of the paper glow like an amber light in Adolph Gottlieb's "Beacon." These are minimalist works, a few marks on paper that demonstrate how a strategically placed line or shape can stand as a thing in itself and, at the same time, affect other lines and shapes.

Joan Mitchell's "Fields I" is simplicity itself. Six horizontal black blobs are evenly spaced over a field of scratchy, loopy, dry brushed lines. But within this surface simplicity of form is an intricate network of marks that are exuberant and spontaneous, yet perfectly balanced — classical order expressed through an explosion of freely drawn marks.

The same kind of complexity-within-simplicity can be seen in Franz Kline's Sumi on paper, "Two Studies for Shenandoah Wall." I don't know if Kline intended these two studies to be displayed in a single, double-cut mat or not. But this is how they are shown, and as such they reverberate beautifully against each other. They are long, horizontal drawings displayed one above the other. The top drawing is done with quick lines that create an abstract representation of movement, as if a freight train is barreling across the surface at 100 miles per hour. The bottom drawing looks like a Japanese sketch of a house. The latter is as placid as the former is fast.

The most complex works, and my favorites, are by Jasper Johns. His "Painting with Two Balls" is a screen print based on one of his famous constructions with two metal balls lodged between two boards. This piece seriously questions the relationship between abstraction and realism. Never known as a great colorist (although I think he is a better colorist than he is given credit for), Johns stretches the limits of black and white here with deep, rich blacks, glowing whites, and delicate grays. His "Corpse and Mirror." is a complicated pattern of chevron shapes in red, yellow, blue and gray painted over a balanced grid that divides the format into equal parts. The patterns take form, and then change direction in surprising ways. Just when you think you see the overall pattern, it changes.

If I entered the gallery with a sense of quietude, I left convinced that I had, indeed, been in the presence of greatness. Yet I also carried away a slight feeling of disappointment. I was let down by the two Pollock drip paintings. They were blobby. The ink looked dead on the old brown newsprint, and there were none of the lacy intricacies that we see in the best of his drip paintings. I was also disappointed that there were no works by Willem de Kooning, and I seemed to have completely overlooked the Lee Krasner, which was listed, but I don't recall seeing. And I thought the two Robert Rauschenberg lithographs were boring. More and more his prints look like commercial illustration. These were minor disappointments. All in all, "The New York School: The Politics of Abstraction" is a show that should be seen and seen again.

*Author's note: This exhibition took place in the old Tacoma Art Museum, which was housed in a three-story bank building. Would the feeling of quietude have been the same if it had been shown in the new Tacoma Art Museum? I do not know.*

## Sandy Skoglund

# Breathing glass

*The Weekly Volcano, Feb. 19, 2004*

Sandy Skoglund first gained national fame as a photographer of odd scenes in which it is hard to tell if the environments are real or constructed. Oddly colored squirrels and foxes invade interior scenes that look like stage sets, but which could just as well be actual rooms that have been painted — and I mean really painted: walls, ceilings and furniture all painted one solid color. The people and animals in Skoglund's environments look real, but they have been painted blue or red or green. Perhaps they are stuffed animals or plaster figures or dolls.

Since there is little inside the frame to give a sense of scale, the teetering balance between reality and unreality is heightened — most emphatically so when people are included in the scenes, because the people are undeniably real live models — except when they are undeniably not. Confusing? You bet. And that's the charm of a Skoglund photograph.

Skoglund is now equally recognized as an installation artist because the sets she constructs for her photographs stand alone as works of art.

Two of her installations, along with a photograph taken from each, can be seen at the Museum of Glass. Each installation is approximately 15 feet in height, width and depth, and consists of a backdrop panel, floor and constructed figures.

"Breathing Glass" is a world of brilliant blue. The blue backdrop is covered with thousands of fluttery glass dragonflies and marshmallows. The floor is made of inlaid blue glass tiles in a crackle pattern approximately six inches below a clear glass sheet. Attached to the glass sheet on thin wire rods are hundreds of tiny human figures. Three life-size human figures dive into this environment. Made of glass tiles in a pattern matching that of the floor, these figures are upside-down, resting on their heads, as if this blue environment is water they have just plunged into (like an underwater scene as viewed through glass) or space without gravity within which they float.

The most wonderful thing about this piece is the way it plays with illusions of depth. In the figures, for instance, the white lines and blue planes are clearly on different levels, but are there blue glass chips on white plaster figures or white lines appliquéd on blue glass figures?

"Raining Popcorn" is an all-white environment made entirely of popcorn and looking more like a blizzard than the rain storm of the title. Two men and a wolf stand around a fire by a snow-covered tree. The men and the wolf are sculpted figures that are completely covered with popcorn.

Both pieces are motorized. Every 15 minutes the motors turn on and the backgrounds shimmer and shake. It's an interesting if somewhat gimmicky effect.

The photographs are far more effective and less stagy than the installations. But comparing them is fascinating. In the "Raining Popcorn" installation, there is one tree, but in the photograph there are two. In the installation, sticks are stacked for a fire but there are no flames. But in the photograph, the fire burns bright. And in the photograph three human models join the two sculpted figures to create a tableau with narrative implications best left to the viewer's imagination. In the "Breathing Glass" installation, the people are upside-down. In the photograph, the whole set is turned upside down, and now the live models are diving down and the glass figures are standing; and the floor becomes the surface of a swimming pool as seen from under the water.

A museum statement about "Breathing Glass" may have said it best: "the installation and its photograph suggest that truth may be as elusive as creativity itself."

# Morris Graves: Instruments for a New Navigation

*Art Access, August 2000*

Mention the name Morris Graves and images immediately spring to mind: flat, unmodulated landscapes with birds or moons or snakes, soft and mysterious with a minimum of detail. Seldom does the name evoke images of sculpture, because Graves is famous for painting and virtually unknown as a sculptor. In 1962, however, he created a large body of strangely beautiful, totemic sculptures in steel, brass, marble and glass. This body of work, called "Instruments for a New Navigation," was inspired by the NASA space missions then in their infancy. They were further inspired by looking at celestial bodies through telescopes and through having studied concepts of metaphysical unity, especially Asian philosophies. These sculptures are elegant, totemic objects that invite introspection and embody Graves's quest for wholeness.

Forty years after creating these pieces, 90 years old and living in semi-retirement in California, Graves reassembled them, and now they are being shown for the first time in an exhibition that started in New York and has traveled to Tacoma. The exhibition features a large number of these odd, fantasy instruments arrayed on tables, and the sculpture is complemented by a group of paintings from the late 1930s to the early 1990s.

Grace Gleuck, writing for the New York Times, was less than laudatory in her critique of these sculptures when the show opened at Schmitt-Bingham Gallery in New York. "But alas," Gleuck wrote of the sculpture, "their whimsical mix of pseudoscience and philosophical pretensions, their ungainly position between sculpture and painting, doesn't work well. At best these objects are high decoration, a far cry from the delicate mysteries of Mr. Graves's luminous paintings at their best."

I beg to differ. These sculptures have all the beauty, mystery, elegance and timelessness of Graves's best paintings. In fact, in this show the paintings suffer in comparison with the sculpture. With about three marvelous exceptions, these are not among the best of Graves's paintings. Most of them are tedious in their overworked detail and refinement of surface. They are too superficially pretty and nothing like the work for which Graves is most famous. Furthermore, his famous luminosity is lost, as many of these works on paper have faded (they look much better in reproduction than "in the flesh").

The sculptures, on the other hand, have a timeless quality with their references to both celestial and sea navigation, to stars, compasses, telescopes and magical instruments. They connect ancient arts with modern science and religious yearnings, and they are made of materials that will never fade. In fact, they look amazingly contemporary considering they were done in the early '60s (they probably would not have received a warm reception had they been shown back then).

Each piece is a variation on the same basic form: a disc or plaque in cast bronze or marble with materials such as glass and mirrors on top of rods of nickel-plated bronze on marble bases, and they are grouped together like instruments in some mysterious future control room — or maybe a science lab from an ancient fabled city such as Atlantis.

"Weather Prediction Instruments for Meteorologists" has three discs arranged in ascending order of size atop crosslike rods on marble bases. The front and largest disc contains sheets of clear glass that sandwich globs of bronze slag that looks like a floating clump of sea grass. Behind it is a larger disc that is a sheet of gray marble with a hole in the center. On the rod that holds this disc is a small fan blade colored a very light oxidized blue, and behind it is the largest disc, this one a sheet of translucent glass in a dark blue-green hue. It is designed, as most of these pieces are, to be looked through, not at. The colors and striations of markings are beautiful, and they change according to the light and the position of the viewer.

"For the Study of Ultraviolet Light Healing" is square in format with a central grid of rectangular glass pieces hinged together on a luminescent mauvish red ground. "The Opposite of Life is Not Death; The Opposite of Life is Time" is a circular slice of alabaster framed in nickel-plated brass and mounted on a brass post. Graves has cut an open circle and inserted a tiny hour glass. The hour glass lies on its side, meaning the sand will never move; time will never change.

"Instrument for a New Navigation" is a brass disc atop a pole with three faucet-like protuberances along its circumference, looking somewhat like an ancient ship's wheel. The brass disc holds a blue marble sheet that looks like stars and celestial clouds in a blue sky. A hole drilled in the center of this disc contains a lens through which can be seen Graves's painting "Waning Moon" on the back wall (also reflected in this lens are Dale Chihuly vases along the opposite wall, an added bonus you'll get at TAM and nowhere else).

"Waning Moon" is one of the best of the paintings in the show. On a black ground of crinkled paper is a pair of two-headed eels that come together to form an elliptical yin-yang symbol. Above this are black and gray linear markings that look like a hovering insect with spindly legs. Two tiny white dots near the top are like eyes glowing in the dark.

Other powerful paintings are "Night Sky #1," which reflects the disc shapes so prevalent in the sculpture, and "A Tantra-Yantra Image, India," which is a playful image of two phallic shapes in black line on a red-splattered ground.

Willie Ray Parish

# Humpbacks and crossroads

*Art Access, March 1998*

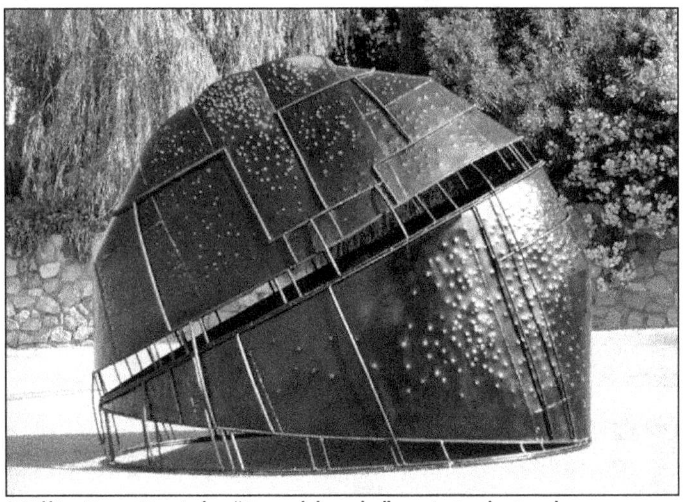

*Willie Ray Parish, "Breakback," painted steel, 6'x8'x5' reproduced by permission of the artist*

From El Paso, Texas, comes Willie Ray Parish with an exhibition of sculpture at Bryan Ohno Gallery that looks as if it were tailor made for the Pacific Northwest. A solid sculptor who knows his way around metal and wood, Parish is gradually and belatedly gaining a much-deserved national reputation.

The exhibition serves as a kind of mini-retrospective highlighting works from two distinct periods: the "Humpback" series, variations of shapes formed by surfacing sea mammals, and a group of wooden sculptures and wood and steel assemblages that relate well to each other even though each piece explores different ideas. The works in this series are metaphors for various life experiences. The titles imply their meaning: "Crossroads," "Carcass" and "Divider," communicating universal themes while leaving room for the individual's interpretation.

"Divider" creates a massive Z shape on the floor. Built of oak timbers with hand-carved wooden joints, it is like a dormant but threatening snake that may rise up at any moment. Parish thinks of it as a barrier, a metaphor for the barriers we face daily in life. A similar piece, "Crossroads," carries a related metaphorical weight — the decisions we must make at life's crossroads. This piece is a vertical X that meets at a point at the top. It is assembled out of columns from an old home in Mississippi. Parish's Southern heritage shows up in many ways, from found materials saved from his Mississippi home to naming a piece "Humpback: Rolo" after a teammate on a bygone Ole Miss Rebel football team.

During his long career, Parish has done a little of everything, from environmental and earthwork pieces to installations wherein he cuts out part of the gallery floor, to massive-minimalist abstractions, to traditional ceramic vessels. His humpback series is probably the nearest thing to a unified body of work he has ever produced, and I find this series to be by far his most exciting.

Although the forms of whales and dolphin and manatees rising out of the sea are familiar enough, the works should primarily be viewed as abstract. There is no attempt at realism. The forms are, by design, vague enough that viewers might respond to them as aeronautical or as something other than sea mammals. The simple shapes are enhanced with subtle but striking surface variations, as Parish hammers, polishes and paints the surface with layers of enamel, hand-polishing each layer until the sculptures almost become paintings.

"Humpback: Nature Girl" and "Humpback: Rolo" rise ominously from the floor, looking much larger than their actual size (3' x 7' x 3'). The rough skins are made of welded stainless steel and the surface scarring is made by hammering the inside with a ball peen hammer. The shapes are rough but elegant. He thinks of the surfaces as representing the scars of life in the sea with natural predators or the breakdown from environmental toxins. But his minimalist forms and the care taken with surface treatment elevate form above content.

The later works in particular are almost too pretty for the metaphorical weight they carry. The surfaces look almost like paintings by Jules Olitski or Larry Poons. In the long run these dichotomies (rough/smooth, abstract/symbolic) may be the best things these sculptures have going for them.

The smaller pieces in the Humpback series hang on the wall, and the vertical orientation changes the associations from mammals to something more akin to shields or, perhaps, even sea shells. The raw surfaces become more jewel-like, as in "Manatee," which is painted white with hundreds of pebble-like protrusions that are painted red and blue. The elegance of this piece is starkly beautiful.

Parish started this series out of concern for the environment and selected sea mammals as a symbol for his attempt to call attention to environmental crises. "The shape formed by the portion of a mammal that breaks above the water is both beautiful and mysterious," Parish says. "There are an infinite number of variations to this simple form and the mystery of what we don't see is so powerful."

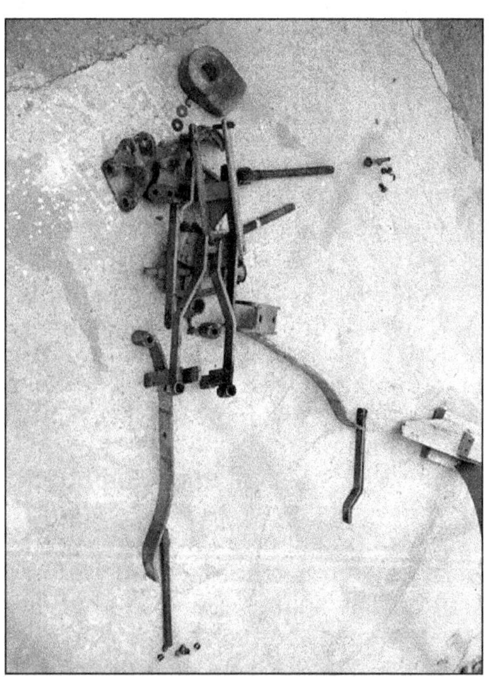

*Willie Ray Parish, "Bad Crossing," found metal, reproduced by permission of the artist*

Over the past decade Parish's work has changed considerably. He has done large-scale installation pieces based on memories of growing up in Mississippi; suspended sculptures with the smooth sweep of an airplane wing based on dim memories of his grandfather who was a pilot in the 1940s.

Now he says that his work has evolved, or devolved as he phrases it, to one or two approaches. "When the work is to be shown at a university or an educational institution I usually do an installation. The installations are conceptually based, non-object, and possibly post-modern. I'm currently working on a group of figurative pieces that consist of old steel parts that are placed to resemble human remains after a degree of decomposition. The parts are not welded or attached. They are my tribute to the hundreds of people who die every year crossing the desert in search of a better life.

"Bad Crossing," one of the "human remains" sculptures, looks at first sight like an almost random collection of discarded metal machine parts. But discerning viewers can see that it forms the image of a decomposing body left in the desert near the Mexican border where Parish says approximately 300 bodies a year are found.

Parish and his wife, the painter Becky Hendrick, run the Border Art Residency in La Union, New Mexico near the border between old and New Mexico.

Thornton Willis

# A Painter's Painter

*The Weekly Volcano, Jan. 8, 2004*

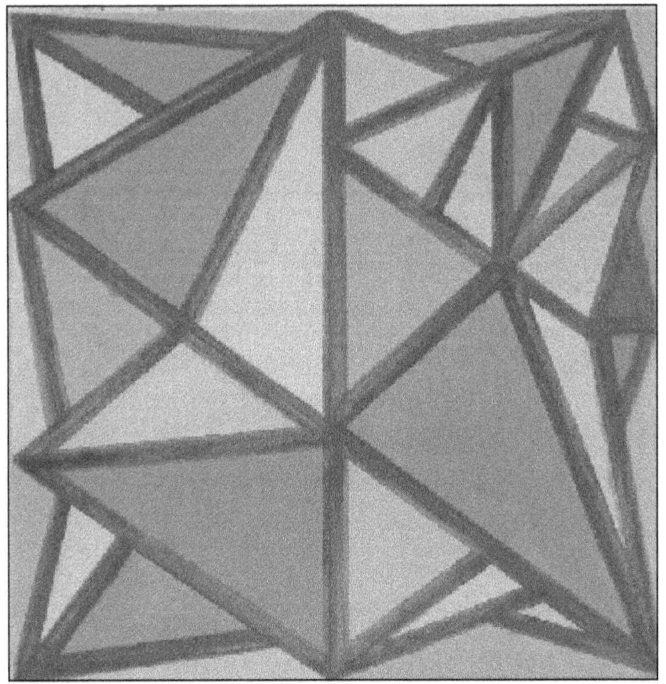

*Thornton Willis, "Spinner" oil on canvas, 96"x72", 2003, photo by Tom Evans*

While surfing the Web recently, I came across a site with work by the painter Thornton Willis. Willis is an old friend, but I had not seen him since 1986, and the last time I had seen him prior to that was in 1968. He was my mentor back then. It was my senior year in college and his first year as a teacher. We shared a studio and he taught me things about painting — mostly by example — that I had never imagined, instilling in me a love for the purity of paint with its variety of surface qualities.

Willis left our little college down South in the late '60s, after only one year on the faculty. He went to New York, where he fought to gain acceptance in the glitzy world of art galleries. Gradually he succeeded. By the early '80s he had become famous in a small way. His paintings were shown in major museums and galleries throughout the world, and articles were written about him in all of the major art magazines.

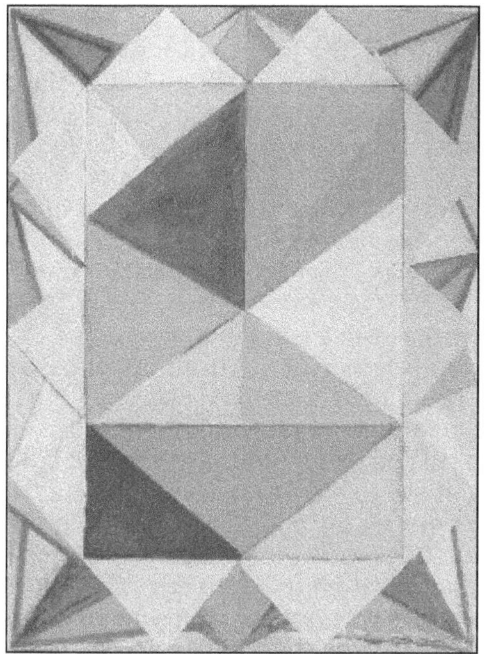

*Thornton Willis, "By Four" oil on linen, 28"x28", photo by Tom Evans*

More than one critic referred to him as a painter's painter and spoke of how younger artists looked up to him. He was admired for the purity of his work. His paintings consisted of simple shapes in often-brilliant colors. His forms were minimalist: stripes or bands of color in the late '60s and early '70s, a single, monumental wedge shape in the mid-'70s, zigzags in the early '80s and rectangular grids after that. Stylistically his paintings synthesized the formal elements of the Russian Constructivists, Piet Mondrian and early Frank Stella with the intense and sloppy paint application of Abstract Expressionism.

In the late '80s, Willis almost vanished from the art scene. It's a fickle scene, and for no apparent reason he fell out of favor. His name quit showing up in the art magazines. I lost contact with him and did not see anything about him in print for ten years. But when I found his Web site, I discovered that he had never given up and that his latest paintings are his strongest yet.

In his latest works, his rectangular grids have morphed into architectonic constructions of triangular shapes that create the illusion of pushing out from the surface of the canvas. These paintings are weighty with volume.

In many ways, the history of twentieth century painting was a history of the depiction of space on a two-dimensional surface. The Renaissance tradition of paintings with illusions of deep space through perspective gave way at the beginning of the twentieth century to Cubistic planes, which gave way to flat surfaces with no depth, which was supplanted by a new kind of space that expands visually beyond the flat surface. Frank Stella, the master of this new kind of expansionist space, traces it back, ironically perhaps, to a Renaissance painter, Carravagio.[1]

I know that Willis is a great admirer of Stella, but I have no way of knowing whether or not his more expansive space is a direct result of studying Stella's ideas.

Willis's formal structures are a mixture of careful planning and intuition. His color schemes are very thoughtful in that each painting is uniform in either intensity or value. No one could have chosen colors more carefully, yet his painting method implies that his choices were arrived at intuitively in process rather than through calculation, as if through trial and error he adjusted his colors until he finally got them just right. And in the best Abstract-Expressionist tradition, his brushstrokes leave a visual record of his struggles as he layers, wipes out and re-paints. Like the scars and wrinkles that lend character to an old man's face, the rough, viscous and layered surface of Willis's paintings speak of a lifetime love affair with paint and canvas from a man who continues to be a painter's painter.

1 - Stella's complicated theories of the use of space in painting are explained in his book *Working Space*.

## Bill Viola

# Motion and Mysticism

*Art Access, July-August 2002*

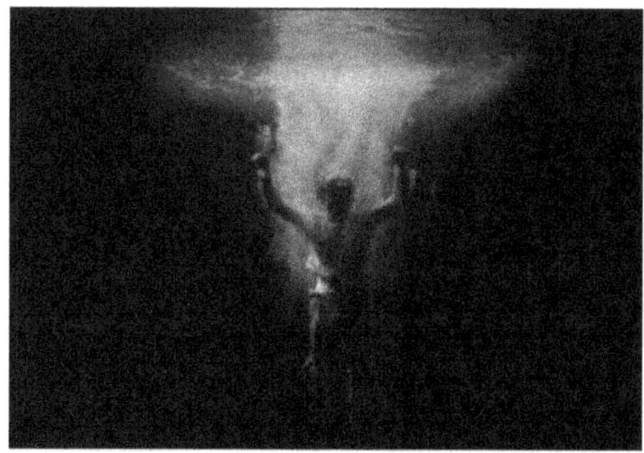

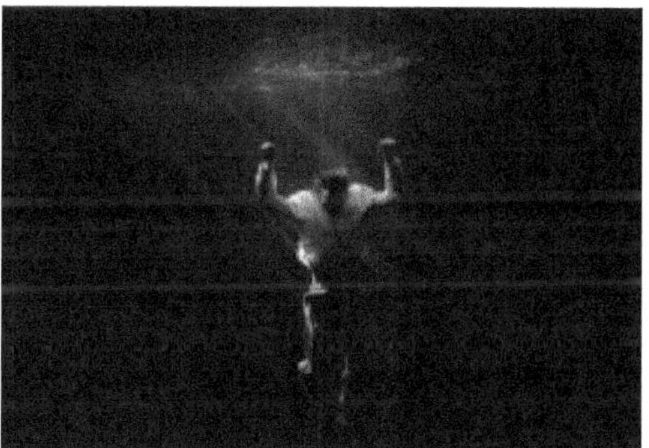

*Video clips from Bill Viola's "Ascension"*
*Photo courtesy Tacoma Art Museum*

To say that Bill Viola is fast eclipsing Nam June Paik as the world's most famous video artist may be a bit of hyperbole, but just a bit. On the other hand, it is certainly no stretch to say he is the hottest young video artist on the scene today. I remember that at the turn of the millennium one of the major art magazines asked a number of artists and critics to pick the artists to watch in the new millennium, and Bill Viola's name came up more than any other (closely followed by Cindy Sherman, if memory serves me right). His videos are part of many museum collections around the world, including the Museum of Modern Art and the Tate Museum. He has received numerous honors, including a John D. and Catherine T. McArthur Award (commonly known as the genius award) and a Getty Research Institute Scholar-in-Residence award. And he represented the United States in the 1995 Venice Biennale.

After seeing images of his work in magazines for years, I have been dying to see them full size and live. Finally we have a chance. The Tacoma Art Museum presents "Bill Viola: Something Above, Beyond, Below, Beneath." This exhibition includes three video works: "Ascension," "Chott el-Djerid (A Portrait in Light and Heat)," and "The Reflecting Pool."

Wall text in the gallery provides critical and historical information on Viola's work, philosophical statements from Viola, and information about the history of video art, and a number of tools to help visitors understand the medium. Included in the wall text is the statement that it is impossible to describe a Bill Viola video. Experientially, philosophically and spiritually this may be true; no amount of description begins to explain a Bill Viola video. But factually they are easy to describe. By way of example, I shall describe one of the three videos in the exhibition, "Ascension."

You step behind a black curtain into a dark and empty room. On a wall-size video screen you see a figure of a man underwater, his arms outstretched, elbows bent, as if in supplication. His clothes billow out. There is very little color. The water, a dark blue; his clothes a dull off-white; bubbles silvery as stars at night; rays of white light beaming in from the top left side of the screen. Is the man dead or alive? It is impossible to tell. He does not move, but the water moves him. He remains under water and motionless longer than would seem to be humanly possible, but this can be accounted for by the editing process, or it could be an illusion of lengthened time created by the video's hypnotic quality.

Bubbles ascend as light flows downward. The figure rises ever so slowly. Bubbles and figure move at the same snail's pace. There is sound, impossible to describe but vaguely reminiscent of the songs of whales. It is a symphony of light, sound and movement with the kind of repetitive pace one associates with a Phillip Glass composition.

The figure rises until his head reaches the surface of the water. Then he sinks until he disappears below the bottom of the screen. The speed at which the figure moves matches the speed of the bubbles, which matches the tempo of the sound track. When the figure vanishes there is nothing left but rising bubbles, light and sound. The quiet is loud. Sound seems to fade. The viewer is lulled almost to sleep. Then suddenly the figure plunges into the water again with a shocking explosion of light, sound and movement, as the video loops again and again.

Similar themes and techniques can be seen in "The Reflecting Pool." In it a man walks out of a forest and stops by a body of water. He jumps, and time stops. The image is seen as reflected in the pool. After a moment, the man emerges from the water without ever having fallen in. (If that description doesn't make sense, that illustrates the truth of the claim that Viola videos are impossible to describe.)

By carefully crafting sequences of images and sounds, Viola produces videos that hint at the enormity of our world and the human condition beyond what we see in front of us. He zooms in and out of vast landscapes, focuses on details, slows or speeds up time, and juxtaposes different scenes, urging viewers to trust their intuition and discover multiple levels of awareness in the world. Everything in a Viola video presents a balance of opposites. What comes to mind is placid violence, an obvious contradiction in terms.

His subjects have to do with the basic elements of earth, air, fire and water; and humankind's interaction with these elements over time. Perhaps we should not so much analyze or even think about his work as simply experience it

# A few hours in the Frye with Joseph Park and Phillip Pearlstein

*A compilation of articles in Art Access and the Weekly Volcano 2005*

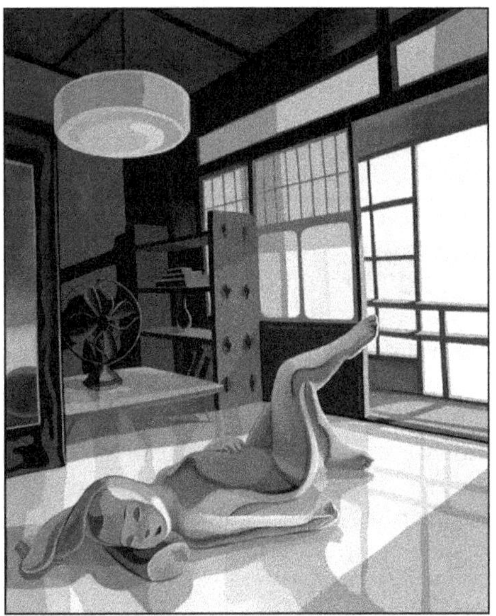

*Joseph Park, "La Belle" 52"x43," oil on linen, 2002*

A few hours in the Frye Art Museum is worth the drive to Seattle. And it is one of the few museums anywhere with no admission fee.

I had some slight reservations about their current featured exhibition, "Joseph Park: Moon Beam Caress," but they are reservations of a type that make me want to go back and look again and again, until I can figure out what he's all about.[1]

I'll admit that I was dismissive of Park's work at first glance. But I went back for a second look, and now I'm studying his work in the exhibition catalog, and I admit that I don't know what to think. Perhaps he is a paradigm of post-modernist sensibility, or maybe he's just a charlatan or trickster whose paintings should be on humorous greeting cards rather than in a prestigious museum.

Joseph Park paints pictures that look like storybook illustrations or still frames from animated films. They fall loosely within the genre of Pop Surrealism. But that would be Pop Surrealism a la Walt Disney. His paintings are bizarre, cleverly humorous and sweetly romantic; and his technique is flawless (the paintings are almost too smooth to have been done by hand, but they were). He paints anthropomorphic animals with a cute and slick look like Hello Kitty and Japanese anime. His interior and exterior scenes are full of moonlight and shadows. And he ransacks the history of film and art for inspiration. There is also a lot of sex, but it is all implied rather than blatant and could easily get a G rating.

There are two paintings that are take-offs on paintings by the great 19th century French painter Jean-Auguste-Dominique Ingres. "La Grande Odalisque is patterned after Ingres' "Odalisque" and "Bather" is patterned after Ingres' "The Valpincon Bather." But in Park's "Odalisque" the reclining nude is an elephant with a woman's body, and in "Bather" the voluptuous nude with her back turned (Ingres loved women's backs) is a cuddly bunny rabbit with a woman's body.

Many of his paintings are sepia toned. Others are predominantly monochromatic in rich, burning reds or deep blues. His scenes are always theatrically staged, and the lighting is always artificial. And there is foreboding mystery underneath much of his romantic sweetness.

"Honorific" is a painting of a horse with an oversize head and mane, all in tones of Venetian red and brown, light beams splaying out from behind his head — all sweetness and light, but the expression in the horse's beady eyes is malevolent.

"La Belle" is a painting of a rabbit woman reclining on the floor of a spare modern apartment with sunlight streaming in a la Edward Hopper. Her bunny rabbit ears are twisted like a French bun in mimicry of a woman's hair. She should be, perhaps, a cat instead of a rabbit; because she is clearly a sex kitten. But is she clothed or nude? Like many of Park's nudes she seems to be wearing some kind of body stocking. She appears to be nude but there are no nipples, no navel, no pubic hair — perhaps in parody of paintings from an earlier time in which pubic areas were smooth mounds of flesh.

In Park's paintings the most innocent of figures become sinister, and images that are threatening or provocative appear as soft and cuddly as teddy bears.

Park, who was born in Canada and now lives in Seattle, is a hot commodity right now. He is in style and of the moment. Pearlstein is just the opposite, a staid modern master whose fame has been established for half a century. It would be hard to imagine any two artists more different, but once you get beyond their subject matter you can easily see that they have a lot in common. Both paint passionate subjects with cool detachment; and both are consummate craftsmen.

At first glance I saw Park's humorous paintings of bunny rabbits and elephants riding subways and ironing clothes and lounging in voluptuous poses like human seductresses as merely cute, not really funny. And I saw the mysterious and romantic scenes with moonlight and water and beams of light pouring through trees as sentimental tripe. But I'm beginning to see Park in a different light (no pun intended). I began to think that maybe he is using the cute imagery and clever gags in the way the early Pop artists used advertising imagery. I began to think that maybe Park is a direct descendant of Roy Lichtenstein and Andy Warhol.

## ... and Pearlstein

Also showing at the Frye is Phillip Pearlstein.

Pearlstein is an unqualified modern master and one of the best of the photo-realist painters. His figure drawings may be typical studio nudes, but they are as beautifully drawn and perfectly composed as any you will see anywhere. Seldom if ever have I seen anyone draw with such a sure hand. And he makes of the human figure something purely abstract without losing any of the anatomical correctness of his drawing. The way he uses shadows, patterns in background objects and groupings of muscle and bone mass to create shapes within shapes without changing the realistic depiction of the figure is truly masterful.

Coming out of an Abstract Expressionist tradition in the 1950s, he turned away from abstraction and made a name for himself by painting the most academic of all subjects, nude models posing in studio settings. But he handled his nudes in ways no one else did. He made no attempt to beautify or idealize his models, but showed them with all their blemishes, including cellulite, sagging breasts, optical distortions and perspectival anomalies.

Pearlstein's paintings are familiar because of countless reproductions in magazines over the last half century, but his drawings have not been so widely reproduced, and they often provide a clearer picture of what he is doing visually than do the paintings, which tend to overwhelm due to their naked realism and convoluted patterning.

What comes across more clearly in the drawings is what a sure hand he has. His contour lines are unbelievably strong. In the earliest drawings there are sketchy contours, but in all the later ones the contours are delineated with long strokes covering large sections of the body. No matter how closely you study these drawings you cannot see any indication of a false start or a correction.

Pearlstein's figure drawings may be typical studio nudes, but they are as beautifully drawn and perfectly composed as any you will see anywhere.

1 - I should make it clear that I am no longer as hesitant in my view of Park's work as I was when I wrote this review. His paintings exemplify what I spoke of earlier when I said that art that is off-putting at first glance often proves to be better than art that has an immediate appeal.

# Regional artists, not regional art

I grew up in the Deep South, went to college in Mississippi and graduate school in Tennessee, spent five years in New York, and returned to my home town of Hattiesburg, Mississippi, where I first began writing art reviews for *Mississippi Arts & Letters*, a magazine my wife and I co-published.

Admittedly, Hattiesburg is not the art capital of the world, but I knew artists there who were just as good as any in New York or Los Angeles, including some who moved to those "real" art capitals and were very successful.

Now I live in a small town sixty miles south of Seattle and review shows in markets that are not much more "big time" than where I started. But I know that the only difference between the better artists in these smaller markets and those in New York is that work shown in New York may be seen by more people — more importantly, by wealthier and more influential people.

In other words, there is no longer any such thing as regional art, only regional artists.

The next section begins with a somewhat tongue-in-cheek essay that I call "Seattle Grunge Art," an attempt to find some kind uniformity in Seattle-area art that clearly does not exist in any real way. The reviews that follow it look at regional artists in the Pacific Northwest. As with regional artists in any other part of the world, it is highly unlikely that any of them will ever be famous, but that does not make them lesser artists. I am happy to be able to include them in the same book as Vincent van Gogh and Stuart Davis and Robert Motherwell.

# Seattle grunge art

*The Weekly Volcano, August 2002*

There's a certain look to so much of the painting coming out of Seattle and the Pacific Northwest that it could be seen as a whole new movement, if it only had a name. If some savvy art critic (with more cachet than I and a national reputation to boot) were to name it, it would go down in history along with such movements as Pop Art and Color Field Painting. I call it Seattle Grunge art because it began to show up about the same time as the music of the same name and attitudinally and stylistically has a lot in common with grunge music. You might even think of it as the Ragged Pendleton Shirt School of Painting.

Grunge artists from the Seattle area include Fay Jones, Gaylen Hansen, James Martin, Michael Brophy, Gene Gentry McMahon and C. Blake Haygood. Seen in the recent South Sound exhibition in nearby Tacoma were emerging Grunge artists Hannah Corbett, Katie Baldwin, Greg Lukens and Chauney Peck. Historic precedents for Grunge can be found in the works of Cy Twombly, Susan Rothenberg, Jean-Michel Basquiat, Leon Golub, Phillip Guston and Jim Nutt. Of course none of these people know they are Grunge artists because that critic with cachet hasn't come along to tell them so. But listen up, folks, I'm telling you now.

There seem to be two branches of Grunge art. One branch is typified by colored-in drawings in a cartoon style and relates historically to painters such as Nutt and Basquiat. The other branch is more painterly and relates historically to Rothenberg and Guston. What both branches have in common is a working-class look to paintings that eschew any sense of elegance and thumb their noses at ... well, just about everything and everybody.

More than anything, Grunge is an attitude characterized by sarcastic and twisted humor, and outrage over social injustice and environmental destruction, although these messages are often hidden within highly personal symbolism and iconography. Stylistically Grunge can be abstract or figurative, but it leans more toward the figurative and narrative. The figures often look like cartoons; common images include fantastic machines, instruments of war and vintage vehicles. Haygood, for instance, draws fantasy machines of his own invention that look as if they may have been used in 1933, and Peck included fighter jets in a large-scale drawing in the South Sound show mentioned above.

Objects in Seattle Grunge paintings seem to exist outside of time. Industrial design combines elements from different time periods; vehicles and machines look old but exist in futuristic scenes. (The film equivalent was Alan Rudolph's *Trouble in Mind*, which was filmed in Seattle but set in a mythical "Rain City" in some non-specific future time wherein everybody drove 1950s automobiles.)

Space is an important consideration in Grunge art, as it is in almost all modern and post-modern art. Figures and objects tend to float or lay flat on the surface. There is little or no perspective, either linear or atmospheric, and the arrangement of objects usually has nothing to do with nature. Houses may be above, on or below the ground; figures can walk on air or water. And things do not necessarily appear smaller as they get farther away. In fact, there seems to be no near or far in Grunge art (but there is in and out). The size and placement of figures and objects and abstract shapes — which take on a life of their own as if they are objects too, simply not recognizable — depend on aesthetic considerations rather than truth to any natural order.

Most Grunge paintings have a strong graphic look. Things are drawn in contour and colored in with little or no modeling. Line is paramount. Heavy lines, delicate lines, staccato lines, and lines as smooth as vapor trails left by the Blue Angels. These Grunge artists really know how to draw. Granted, there is a kind of crudity to much of the drawing that to the untrained eye may look like bad drawing, but most of us learned from Matisse and Picasso how to see the finesse and power within so-called inelegant drawing.

Now you know how to recognize Seattle Grunge art when you see it. When your children see it mentioned in art history texts, you can tell them you knew about Grunge before it even had a name.

Ron Hinson

# Seriously beautiful art

*Reviews of Ron Hinson's painted constructions and other works published in the Weekly Volcano, various issues 2003-2007*

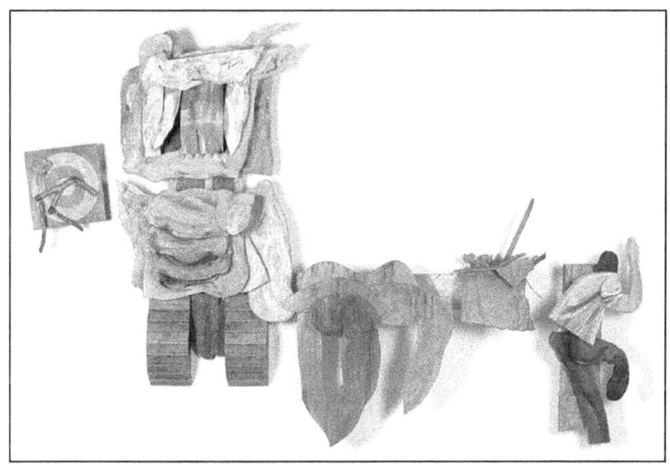

*Ron Hinson, "New Goliath" acrylic on Masonite, wood & plaster, 54"X93"X14"*

*June 2003*

Just when you thought it was safe to go back the art gallery — that is, just when you thought it was safe to assume that anything you're likely to see in a gallery is going to look pretty much like everything else — then along comes Ron Hinson with a group of painted constructions at Childhood's End Gallery in Olympia to prove originality in art is not dead after all. Hinson's work looks like nothing else you're likely to see anywhere. He's the real deal.

There are some other things showing in the gallery: some quilts, some glass art, some turned wood. But alongside Hinson's paintings, they are just so much clash and clutter. They shouldn't be in the same room.

Did I mention that he's the real deal?

Hinson's painted constructions are massive abstract forms that protrude from the wall like hybridized Constructivist and Art Nouveau wall planters. The forms are a combination of flat squares and triangles that jut outward at various angles and biomorphic forms that dance in front of these flatter forms, sometimes in rhythmical patterns and sometimes in seemingly random arrangements that almost — but not quite — defy any sense of harmony or balance. His subject matter is usually derived from sources such as Greek and Roman mythology, classical literature and classical art. But he abstracts his subjects beyond recognition. "These painted constructions do not tell narrative stories," Hinson writes in a statement. "Some of the shapes are 'informed' by images in our visual world, but they do not 'represent' any image. The viewer is encouraged to discern the underlying structure of the visual relationships because in them are encoded the experiences of living."

He does not title his paintings, because he does not want to encourage the viewer to look for narrative content. For Hinson, the aesthetic relationship between visual elements is more important than subject matter. His true subject is not Leda and the swan or the labors of Hercules or the death of Marat. His true subject is color, line, shape, mass, value, pattern and space; and the ways in which all of these visual elements interact. His challenge to himself is to see how far he can push visual boundaries. He stretches the limits of balance and harmony, and he stretches the limits between painting and sculpture. Some of his works have fully-rounded sections that extend a good foot or two from the wall; yet they are paintings, not sculptures. The spatial, textural and color relationships all are dealt with from a painter's point of view, and they are designed to be seen primarily from one side.

Only one painting in the show seemed a little weak to me. It is solid yellow in color. Symmetrically balanced, all of the shapes radiate like encompassing arms from a vertical floral shape in the center. The only variations from the milky yellow color are accents along the edges of shapes, and one circular shape in a yellowish-orange that seems detached from the whole — barely touching on one edge. This one out-of-balance piece teetering on the edge saves it.

Everything else is wonderful. My favorites are the two pieces at the back of the gallery. One consists of four floral shapes in modulated tones of yellow blue, orange and pink that dance in a rhythmical in-and-out pattern over a series of gray triangular shapes. In the very center is a vertical rod painted in stripes of gray. Next to it is a heavy, dense piece that reminds me of sea life, with a flying turtle, fish and two shapes that look like teddy bears. And absurdly extended from the bottom is a tree-limb ladder with pennants on the bottom. It all sounds comically absurd to describe, and there is a comic element, but it is seriously beautiful art.

## From Eden to Steppenwolf

*December 2003*

Ron Hinson's paintings are large, ambitious and complex. They are abstract but with references to forms in nature. Most of them are untitled, but Hinson sometimes makes up titles for his own identification purposes, and these titles often provide clues to the historical and mythological subject matter of his paintings. For instance, in "Eden Theme I," the figures of Adam and Eve are obvious only because of the clue given by the title.

Hinson's painted constructions are elaborately built in sections, mostly out of wood and often built up with massive globs of plaster or acrylic gels and augmented with found materials such as tree branches or scrapings off his palate that are like multi-colored wasp nests. His forms tend to balance contrasting shapes such as free-flowing serpentine shapes on the one hand, and harshly angled squares, rectangles and zigzags on the other. These constructions then become surfaces upon which he paints with highly energetic brushstrokes that are, in turn, contrasted with very precisely painted patterns, so that everything becomes a give-and-take between harmony and contrast.

Aesthetically, Hinson pushes his paintings to the brink of chaos, so that they are almost out of balance. Yet they never quite topple over the edge. (Funny, isn't it? The term "edgy" has become such a hip expression for youthful attitudes, and here we have one of the truly edgy artists in the South Sound, and he's a senior citizen who retired after 39 years teaching art in order to paint full time.)

In addition to his painted constructions, Hinson is showing five earlier pieces called Magic Theaters. In a printed statement, Hinson denies that they refer to the stage, but rather refer to words taken from Herman Hesse's novel "Steppenwolf" to denote a "rather surreal environment." That may be true, but I can't help but think of them as stage sets. The Magic Theaters are rectangular boxes that hang like paintings on the wall. They are approximately four feet long and six inches deep. Inside the boxes are layered curtains or scrims made of wood or canvas, which are backgrounds for such oddities as a swing set with a red velvet cushion, flying pink pea pods and pop-up shooting gallery targets — surreal? Yes, but stage sets nevertheless.

## Art on Center

*February 2007*

If you see Ron Hinson's show at Art on Center Gallery, you might think it is simply a rehash of the show he had there in August 2005. The painted constructions look identical to the ones he showed then. That is, if you don't look too closely or don't remember too clearly. He uses a lot of the same shapes and colors and, in general, mines the same vast vocabulary of visual tropes. Yet, if you were to compare work for work, you'd see great differences.

Likewise, Hinson's acrylic illustrations of children's stories in this show are stylistically identical, in many ways, to his illustrations from Aesop's Fables in his earlier show. He uses a similar palette and similar lyrical lines over a modulated and stippled background, and he brings into play the same kind of humor.

Hinson's painted constructions reference flowers and other plants, and human bodies abstracted beyond recognition. In some areas the surfaces are smooth, and in others they are as craggy as mountain ranges. His paint application has an expressive and loose appearance, but is more highly controlled than it looks.

His paintings pit visual contrasts against one another — contrasts between open and closed forms, between balance and imbalance, chaos and cohesion, unity and variety.

He pushes the edges of controlled chaos so far in some of his painted constructions as to be almost uncomfortable to the viewer. One large painting on the back wall of the gallery (they are all untitled) looked too chaotic to me until I backed up and viewed it from a distance. The top section consists of circular and angular forms in tones of red, yellow and orange, with one feather-like shape (like an old fashioned writing quill) that goes flying off to the right. Large blue shapes below are separated by a bright yellow form. There are curlicues and fans and circles, in a cacophony of colors that jangle the eye when seen up close. But when seen from a distance, every shape leads the eye to another shape.

A smaller construction on the right-hand wall is much more unified in form and color. It is one of my favorites. Organic forms reminiscent of human organs radiate in all directions from a central X-shape made from flat boards painted in broad stripes like a barrier at a railroad crossing. Painted in muted tones of gray and brown, with touches of red and yellow, this is the most cohesive piece in the show, with everything densely compacted into the center.

The largest of his painted constructions dominates the left-hand wall. It is an open design with large spaces between shapes. It looks as if it is ready, at any moment, to fly off the wall in every direction. Hinson has thrown nearly all of his tricks into this one piece. In the center, holding everything together is a large exclamation point of rough wood built up with molding paste or plaster and painted to look like a burnt club or perhaps remnants of some South Seas tribal totem.

When Hinson references narrative in his painted constructions the narratives usually come from classical literature and myth and are abstracted almost, if not completely, beyond recognition. A rare exception is “New Goliath” (reproduced here), which is about modern warfare. No slingshot could ever stop this Goliath.

William Morris

# Object and the Animal

*Art Access, August 2005*

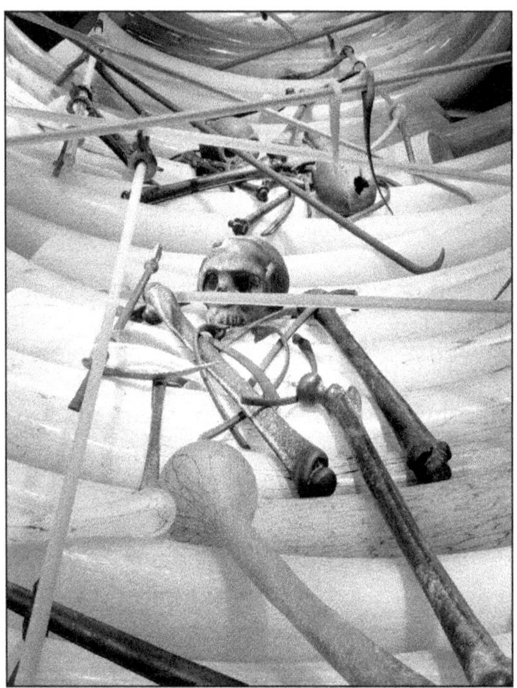

*William Morris, "Cache" (detail), glass, photo courtesy William Morris Studio*

William Morris is a glass artist, but that appellation is not large enough for Morris. Like Dale Chihuly and Benjamin Moore and other stars of the studio glass movement that has become as ubiquitous as rain in the Northwest, Morris comes out of the Pilchuck studio, but other than a meticulous craftsmanship they all share, his work has little in common with any of the other well known Pilchuck artists.

Morris has developed an oeuvre that is idiosyncratic yet universal, evoking ancient magic and mystery. His icons, talismans and imagery consist of anthropomorphic birds (primarily ravens), bones, tusks, funerary urns, skulls both human and animal, and artifacts that look both ancient and contemporary. The surfaces of his objects are usually opaque and heavy looking with, in some instances, a translucence that is barely visible, signifying that, yes, this is glass after all; even though most of his pieces look more like bone, leather, clay or metal than glass.

"William Morris: Object and the Animal, A Mid-Career Survey" at the Museum of Glass in Tacoma is the first major survey of his twenty-year career.

The earliest work in the show is a simple arrangement of three rocks made of highly polished glass with delicate linear veins. Although this piece has the transparency and luminosity usually associated with decorative glass pieces, we see here an early indication of directions Morris takes in later works.

There are representative works from the animals and artifacts of the 1990s that first brought him to wide public attention. These include birds and bird skulls, and two heads of tribal people from indigenous cultures: one a ferocious looking male with dangling skulls for a necklace, and the other a female with an elongated neck adorned with tiny bird skulls. The faces are dull ebony, and the facial structures are hard and bony. Not representing particular people, the woman was inspired by Kenyan women and the man by the ancient Indus people of South Asia. These faces are fierce, proud, handsome and dignified.

"Raven with Skull," 1998, is an excellent example of the countless ravens and crows Morris has done. The form of the bird's head and body is streamlined with the elegance of a Brancusi sculpture, but the abstraction and simplification does not sacrifice realism. Like the Kenyan woman and Indus man, this bird is fierce and handsome. The surface has the look of black stone. The raven is perched on top of a stark white human skull. In its beak it holds a tiny round pot, black with red dots. An identical pot rests in one of the skull's eye sockets. This is a haunting image, mysterious yet real. It is easy to imagine a raven socking away two such pots in the eye sockets of a skull.

There are also three recent large installations, including "Cache," "Artifact Panel," and his most recent installation, "Mazorca."

"Cache" is made up of tusks, approximately the size and shape of elephant or mammoth. They are laid flat on a meal shelf that runs across the entire back wall of the gallery. Scattered in seemingly random patterns on one end of the bed of tusks are bones and skulls. Despite the apparent randomness — as if this is a burial ground accidentally stumbled upon — there are visual patterns that can be discerned when walking around and viewing it from all sides.

"Artifact Panel" is a wall of 369 bowls, urns, horns, skulls, animals and various relics each "pinned" to the wall like specimens in a scientific display. The pins extrude 16 inches from the wall and cast shadows in diamond patterns. Each of the relics, bones, etc. is about the size of a person's hand, and each is a beautiful little jewel in its own right. The entire panel is 32 feet long and almost nine feet high.

"Mazorca," a metaphor for harvest and regeneration, was inspired by South American cultures. The main element is corn — ears of corn measuring four to five feet in length and hanging by heavy ropes from a steel frame. Also hanging from the frame are bones and urns and other forms relating to nature, and standing on the base are large urns, many of which reflect the shape of the ears of corn, with surface patterns that replicate the clustered kernels. In spite of the theme of harvest and regeneration, there is a heavy feeling to this piece, a feeling that it also relates to death.

And death, finally, is an overriding theme to many of the pieces in Morris's oeuvre, most notably in a recent series of cinerary urns he did in 2002 after the death of a family member and in recognition of the loss of lives on September 11, 2001.

CJ Swanson and David N. Goldberg

## Centered on art

*Three reviews in The Weekly Volcano, 2006-2007*

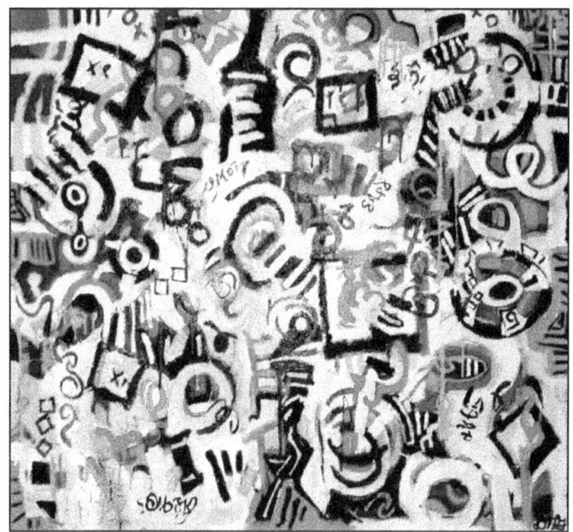

*David N. Goldberg, "Festoon" 44"x48" x 2," acrylic and collage on canvas, photo courtesy a.o.c. gallery*

*April 2006*

I predict that Tacoma's newest art gallery, Art on Center, is going to be successful against all odds. I say "against all odds" because without capital backing and some solid connections with art buyers, it is almost impossible for a contemporary art gallery to succeed, and owners C.J. Swanson and David Goldberg have neither. But what they do have is art-world savvy, good judgment and enthusiasm.

Swanson and Goldberg are Seattle transplants. Both were established artists in Seattle who moved to Tacoma because housing in Seattle has become prohibitive. I spent a good two hours visiting with C.J. yesterday, and I am convinced that she knows what's for real and what's not. The only question is whether or not she knows what will sell. There, time will tell, but I'm impressed with the artists she has lined up for future shows.

Swanson and Goldberg opened their new gallery with a show of their own work. Both paint colorful abstract paintings with circular forms that are evenly distributed across the canvas. Since there are some obvious formal similarities, it is tempting to view their work as being mutually influential, but there are major differences. Swanson's paintings are less abstract. Her forms refer to flowers and pots and organic forms, and they float in shallow space — often overlapping. Goldberg's forms are more abstract and more mechanical in appearance. Rather than floating in shallow space, they are all locked firmly into the same surface plane. Another major difference is their use of color. Although they both use bright, primary colors, Swanson's colors tend to be raw, and Goldberg tones his colors down by placing a lot of neutral tones next to his brighter colors.

Goldberg's paintings have a factory feel and Swanson's come from the kitchen and the garden.

"Spinning Top" by Swanson is a picture of coffee cups, spinning tops, floral shapes and pinch-neck bottles floating on a mostly yellow background. The forms overlap and many are hollow forms delineated by contour drawings. The sizes and shapes of her objects are fairly uniform, and everything flows in a circular motion. In all of her paintings there is a loose structure that is not apparent at first glance. Things look to be free flowing but actually line up in vertical or horizontal bands or in circular motion. In one of her paintings, for instance, there is a vertical band of circles on the left. Next to that is a vertical band of horizontal stripes, and to the right of that are figure-eight shapes drawn with red and pink contour lines, which create more vertical bands.

"Harmonious Quark" by Goldberg is a dense painting of circles, semi-circles, rectangles and triangles jammed together as tightly as a computer circuit board. As in Swanson's "Spinning Top," yellow is the dominant color, but you cannot say the forms are placed on a yellow background, because in Goldberg's paintings it is impossible to tell figure from ground. All of his circles and squares fit together to form larger circles and squares, which in turn divide the canvas in to large vertical and horizontal bands. A group of small squares, stripes and triangles near the top form a horizontal band that is crossed by a more subtle vertical band that divides the canvas into four sections. Similar shapes come together to form five big wheels that dominate the space, and in the upper right hand corner are some marvelous color surprises in dull greens and violets.

These are excellent paintings. Be sure to see them, and make it a point to see what's new at Art on Center every month.

## Barefoot Studio

*Nov. 2005*

Maybe you saw David Goldberg's show at Art on Center last spring. That was just a warm-up for his current show at Barefoot Studios. This show is much bigger, with larger and more vibrant paintings that are more solidly composed.

Goldberg's paintings hark back to the days when modern art was new, when artists like Robert and Sonia Delauny enlivened painting with vibrant abstract forms, when Stuart Davis created the visual equivalent of jazz and Marsden Hartley painted emblematic pictures of German soldiers and Mark Toby's all-over squiggles danced in an explosion of white.

Does this mark Goldberg as outdated and out of touch with contemporary forms? Perhaps. He certainly doesn't seem to be enraptured by the clever imagery that marks much of today's art, and there's nothing shockingly avant-garde about his paintings. But he sure seems to know what painting has been all about since the advent of modern art a century ago.

There are ten new paintings in his latest show, and three older ones. Goldberg paints geometric forms on a flat surface. Circles or discs predominate and are interspersed with triangles, squares, bars of alternating dark and light colors, and various squiggles of paint; and in at least one painting what looks like Chinese calligraphy. There are no obvious or direct references to anything outside the paintings, but it is easy to read industrial forms such as gears into some of the paintings and computer circuit boards into others; and the Chinese writing combined with checkerboard patterns in black and gold could refer to Asian palaces and silk gowns.

The surface forms are in bright colors that look more intense than they really are due to thoughtful juxtaposition of colors. The "backgrounds" of most of his paintings are mostly white and gray, and I put that word in quotation marks because his background shapes tend to advance to the surface plane and become positive rather than negative shapes. The color is laid on in careful strokes of mostly opaque paint of a paste-like consistency that, from one picture to the next, may be heavily built up or watered down — but typically of the same consistency within any one painting.

The hallmark of his paintings is a multiplicity of forms within uniform fields created by repeating similar shapes. By this means, Goldberg brings about variety within unity in individual paintings as well as from painting to painting. For instance, in some of his paintings all of the shapes are of similar sizes, but others have shapes in a great variety of size; in some the paint is thick and crusty and in others it is thin and smooth; some are flat, with everything on the same plane, while others have implied depths. But you never see flatness and depth or thick and watery paint or shapes of the same sizes and shapes of different sizes within the same paintings. This complexity of variety within unity makes it fun to compare his paintings and look for recurring patterns from one to another.

Goldberg employs an interesting use of space. Some paintings are kept flat by placing shapes side by side and having them intersect, and by keeping the values close; while others use overlapping shapes and strong light and dark contrasts, which creates illusions of depth. The difference is clear when you compare "Carnival" and "Karmic Totem."

"Carnival," by the way, is different from all the rest. It is a profusion of small shapes clustered together and fading to emptiness along the edges. More highly energized than any of the other paintings, it is an explosion of circles and drips and squiggles in intense reds and pinks and yellows and blues.

## The Vanity Show

*April 2007*

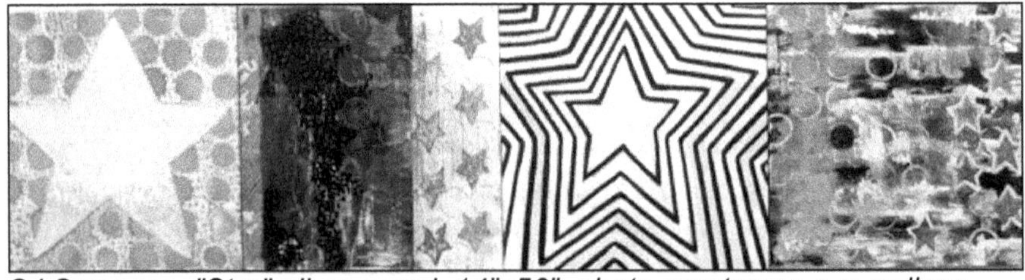

*CJ Swanson, "Star" oil on panel, 14"x56", photo courtesy a.o.c. gallery*

Ah, The Vanity Show. What chutzpah! Art on Center owners C.J. Swanson and David N. Goldberg are showing their own paintings to mark the gallery's second anniversary. This exhibition is an update on Art on Center's premiere show two years ago, which is especially appropriate since this is slated to be the final show in the Center Street space before Swanson and Goldberg move to spacious new quarters on Sixth Avenue in June.

Both of them are damn fine painters. They are partners in marriage and in business, and they share studio space; so similarities in their work should not be surprising. Both are abstract painters. Both display a penchant for repetitive forms in all-over patterns and bright colors. But there are differences as well.

Swanson's paintings are more decorative. Her shapes and lines are more deliberate and more fluid. When not working on her own paintings, she does faux finishing and paints theatrical backdrops, and a lot of carryover from those crafts shows up in her paintings. She is also all over the map from one painting to another. If I didn't know better, I might think four or five different artists are represented by her work. Could it be that she's has multiple personalities? No, she's just very creative and keeps experimenting with new looks and techniques.

Goldberg's paintings, on the other hand, vary almost not at all from one to another. His paintings are more overtly expressive than Swanson's, and most of them are larger. They are gritty and explosive, and the staccato shapes that dance all over his canvases are painted more loosely than his wife's more carefully controlled forms.

Goldberg fills the surface of his canvases with loosely brushed rectangular boxes of flat color — dull, yellow-green, pink, blue, and a brilliant transparent crimson. On top of and into this, he paints circular forms and calligraphic marks. Like Mark Toby and Jackson Pollock — but more jagged than Toby and less fluid than Pollock — he distributes these marks evenly across the surface, giving equal weight to everything. In his two latest paintings, "Festoon" and "Return," he has broken out of this formula and done away with the grid-like underpainting, letting his calligraphic marks float freely in fields of white. I think these two paintings are his best.

The best of Swanson's is a single painting of stars on fields of circular discs called, appropriately, "Star." It is painted on four 14-inch square panels that are put together in a long horizontal her rough and brittle paint application.

# Woven wonders

## Contemporary basket invitational at American Art Company

*The Weekly Volcano, Nov. 6, 2003*

The American Art Company in Tacoma has found a niche market for fine art crafts (once an oxymoron) and filled it admirably with quilts, turned wood and basketry. The gallery's annual turned wood and quilting exhibitions have become mainstays in Tacoma's art scene. The second Annual National Contemporary Basket Invitational features approximately 80 baskets created by both regional and national artists.

To my way of thinking, this show equals the gallery's well established quilt and turned wood shows in both quality and variety of artistic expression. But it has not drawn the big crowds — perhaps because the public thinks of basket weaving as a craft that is severely limited in style. But contemporary basket makers are not limited to traditional forms or materials. Yes, there are baskets woven out of traditional materials such as reeds and vines, but this show includes lace, hog gut, beeswax, glass beads, copper wire, brass, screws and nuts, fish bone, feathers and steel washers. And I saw only one basket with a handle in the whole show, and it looked more like a serving dish than a basket ("Satellite Basket No. 4" by John Rais, steel and iron).

I was pleased to see that two of my favorite local basket artists — Jill Nordfors Clark from Tacoma, and June Kerseg-Hinson from Olympia — were well represented in the show.

Clark's baskets are kept simple and reductive in shape in order to allow greater expression through the textures, colors and translucence of her unusual materials. She works with hog gut, quill-type needles and lace. The hog gut is a pliable material that she keeps in her freezer at home until she is ready to use it. Woven together with other natural materials, it lends to her baskets the look of some kind of strange underwater growth reminiscent of coral. "Line Drawing II" is a simple cylindrical basket. It is tightly woven at the bottom and loosens up toward the top, the linear patterns of the woven gut and lace looping back upon themselves in swirl patterns. In "Rain Dance," a similar cylindrical shape is woven with lace and gut, and shooting up through it are maple reeds that modulate in color from green at the bottom to purple at top. "Urchin II" is a round basket woven with the same combination of lace and gut, and shot through with goose quill toothpicks. The beauty is in the soft color modulations and the translucency of her materials.

Kerseg-Hinson's "Spectre of Elegance" is one of the most impressive pieces in the show due to its brilliance of color and imposing size. Made of magnetic wire and waxed linen, it is in the shape of a woman's body, from her broad shoulders to the tapered hem of her dress. Or perhaps it could be seen as a hanging dress, a stand-in for a missing woman, which seems to fit better with the title. Sixty-two inches high, it hangs on wires from the ceiling and hovers above the floor. The material is tightly woven, giving it the dense look of chain mail; the color is a brilliant red at top that darkens to black at the bottom. Following the tapered form, wires stick out like electrical charges that are sparse at top and dense at bottom.

Another Kerseg-Hinson piece, "Caja Para Suenos II," is a small, open-weave basket made of spun paper, magnet wire, acrylic paint and beads. Square at top and bottom, it rounds out in a bulging middle. Its color scheme is a deceptively simple balance of complementary yellows and purples — deceptive because the interplay of the two colors is much more complicated that it looks at first blush.

Other artists of note include Charissa Brock, Diane Banks, Herman Guetersloh and Gerri Johnson-McMillin.

Diane Kurzyna

## Between Dream and Reality
## White trash wedding

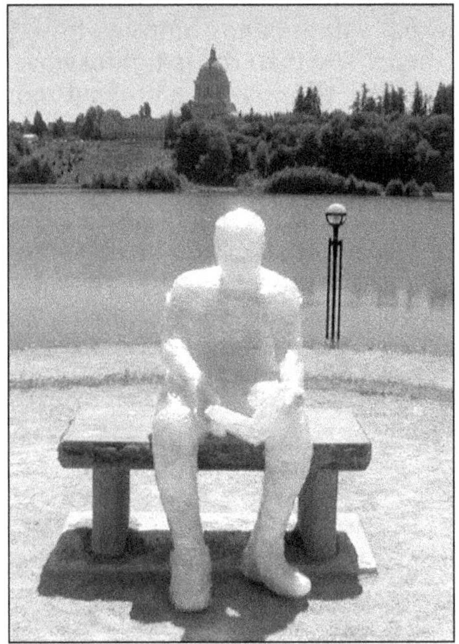

*Diane Kurzyna, plastic wrap figure seated on park bench in front of Olympia state capitol*

*Compiled from various reviews in the Weekly Volcano, 2003-2006, with additional comments for this book*

Here's a name that keeps popping up in this column: Diane Kurzyna, otherwise known as Ruby Recycle the Dumpster Diving Diva. It's almost too late, two more days to be exact, but she has a great, funny and surprisingly educational show at the Art Center Gallery at Seattle Pacific University. The show is called "White Trash Wedding Redux." A title like that is bound to bring to mind trailer parks and shotgun weddings, probably in Arkansas circa 1950. But the "white trash" refers to mostly white materials scavenged from trash bins, and the "redux" means it's been done before (it's a repeat of a show at The Evergreen State College).

In "White Trash Wedding" Kurzyna has created a wedding tableau complete with bride and groom and tiered wedding cake. Everything is made out of junk. The bride is all decked out in the traditional bridal white (white lampshade, white foam wrap, white plastic bag, white plastic netting, white cord, and Red Rose tea tags, which are mostly white). Kurzyna uses junk because she loves the look of it and because she believes in the value of recycling.

Kurzyna is inventive in her use of materials and themes. She often uses materials in ways that carry multiple meanings, such as when she makes faces out of mirrors so the figures become portraits of the viewers. But like all good barbs, hers teach valuable lessons while eliciting belly laughs — lessons about recycling and, in this case, lessons about traditional Jewish weddings.

Now for a personal note: Dear Mrs. Ruby Recycle challenged me to really criticize her work. Well, my dear Ruby, all I can say is I wish you would go more out on a limb, be even more audacious. If you're going to be outlandish, be outlandish. Why make a 12-inch tall woman out of a plastic milk jug when you can use hundreds of jugs and make a bigger than life Jewish bride? Instead of mirrors for faces, why not magnifying mirrors that reflect giant mouths or eyeballs? Instead of simply designing "in the round" (as you do so well), why not put your creatures on revolving platforms or in motorized vehicles? You have a wonderful imagination. Don't be afraid to stretch it to the limit.

*2006-2007*

In a juried show at South Puget Sound Community College in January 2006, Kurzyna showed comical little creatures made from recycled materials with Wonder Bread bodies and mirrors for faces. Her two pieces were called "Wonderful Self-Portrait" and "You Look Wonderful." (How many puns on Wonder Bread can she come up with?) The former is a single figure that hangs on a wire from the ceiling and looks like a puppet on a string; the latter consists of two figures, male and female. They are arranged at ascending heights with the idea that, in order, children, women and men can look into the mirror faces and see themselves.

Jump ahead a few months to the "Java Diva" show that Kurzyna curated for the same college art gallery. She has graduated to life size sculptures of people sculpted in a method she describes as casting in plastic wrap and tape. She wraps her models in plastic wrap and tape, cuts the mold away from the body, reassembles it with tape, and stuffs it with bubble wrap for support.

Seen in this exhibition are one figure from a live model and one from a mannequin. These have a clean and lean look and say more with less than her earlier work. They are reminiscent of and pay homage to George Segal's plaster figures, and like Segal's figures, they are most effective when seen in natural settings such as in the Olympia art event, "Here Today" — public installations by eight different artists.

Here she shows relatively realistic figures of ordinary people engaged in ordinary activities and placed in natural settings such as downtown shop windows, on public benches and on city buses. "My project proposes to straddle that poetic space between dream and reality," Kurzyna states. "...I want to deal directly with scenes and situations familiar to myself and the public, using personal experience and human values to convey a visual art vocabulary that is accessible to the public and still manages to elevate the understanding of art."

Kurzyna's dedication to the use of recycled materials as an act of social responsibility, her championing of other artists who work with recycled materials, and her humor all make for interesting art. But like the Wonder Bread wrappers and plastic wrap she works with, her work is lightweight. Her pieces are conversation starters, but the conversations are like party chatter that touches only lightly on important issues. As an example, there is a piece pictured on Kurzyna's Web site called "Bag Lady in Alley." It is a perky figure of a woman wearing a short skirt and a wide-brimmed hat. Her clothes are made from Wonder Bread bags, thus the pun in the title. I really love this picture, but it's cotton candy for the eye. This lady is saucy and jovial, and poses like a fashion model in front of a colorful graffiti wall. It has more in common with window displays than with high art, and the clever title is a double entendre that refers (once again) to Wonder Bread and to homeless women, who are often called bag ladies. But the high-fashion look is out of keeping with such heavy subject matter.

On the other hand, the reader pictured here was temporarily displayed in various public spaces. His slump-shouldered stance, lack of color and detail, and the placement in unexpected places such as a city bus and a park bench all add up to a work of much greater substance than the bag lady or any of her earlier pieces. In this work there are hints of directions I would like to see Kurzyna push her work.

## Ross Palmer Beecher

# Americana and America's best

*Art Access, May 2003*

Visiting Ross Palmer Beecher's home and studio was a wonderful treat that confirmed what viewing her art had suggested: that her brand of folk-inspired art is as authentic as it seems — which is extremely ironic in light of the fact that Beecher is a 40-something white woman whose art looks like something made by an 80-year-old black man from the backwoods of Alabama.

Beecher has been an admirer of American folk art in general and Southern black folk art in particular since her days as a student at the Rhode Island School of Design, and over the past 20-odd years she has taken elements of those traditions and combined them with influences from Mad Magazine, Andy Warhol and Jasper Johns to come up with an art that is uniquely her own.

Beecher moved to Seattle in 1979, and went to work supporting herself by doing political cartoons at the Pike Place market and selling them for $7 each. Shortly after settling in Seattle, she made a traditional quilt out of cut tin from old cans an artist friend had collected and given to her. With this, she started making the kind of art she continues to make today: quilts, flags and famous folk, which is the name of her latest show at Greg Kucera Gallery. The show will include a number of quirky and humorous, but nevertheless traditional quilts, made out of such common objects as cut tin, pieces of kitchen implements, candy wrappers, and other found and/or cheaply purchased items. Also included will be a number of sculptural heads of famous people from American history such as Jackie Kennedy, Eleanor Roosevelt, Martin Luther King Jr. and Abraham Lincoln. And American flags.

An American flag draped in the front window welcomes visitors to Beecher's house, and although I don't know how to describe the difference, it is most definitely a flag such as you might have seen used as a curtain in some hippy digs from the '60s rather than a flag such as might fly today as a symbol of support for American troops in Iraq. Inside her house there are more flags, many incorporated into works of art. And the art is everywhere: hanging from walls, draped over tables, cluttering the kitchen cabinets, stacked on furniture. It is hard to tell the art from the assorted bric-a-brac Beecher has collected, which one just knows will eventually wind up as part of a work of art.

Hanging from an easel in the dining room is "Cobweb Candy Quilt Study," one of Beecher's traditional quilts made from copper, tin, glass, candy and found objects. All in shiny copper and gold colors, including gold and silver candy wrappers, the pattern is regular and repetitive in a traditional manner. Beecher said it was a nod to Northwest traditional quilting and to folk art from the Deep South. It reminded me of Claes Oldenburg's early soft sculpture, only in reverse, in that the hardness of the material makes it unusable as a quilt just as the softness of Oldenburg's toilet and drum set made them unusable. It seems to shout, "I may be a quilt, but you can't wrap yourself in me!" Or, to put it another way, this quilt is to traditional quilts what Renee Magritte's "Ceci n'est pas une pipe" was to a traditional pipe. The center element of almost every square is a piece of candy, still in its foil wrapper but treated to hold its shape. There are mini-Hershey bars and Reese's Pieces, and Halloween candies from Fred Meyer's. Continuing the pattern but breaking up the bronze and gold color scheme are pieces of colored glass, as in stained glass windows. This is one of a group of quilts to be included in the show.

Also to be included, and scattered all over the house, were her funky portraits of American history figures such as "Jackie O" with a dead-serious look on her face, made of a black vinyl purse, metal, parts of a cheese grater and other scrap cooking ware from the '50s, and the stereotypical Jackie Kennedy pillbox hat made from an old pot with a wooden knob on top (connected by two sticks that swivel, Jackie can tip her hat). Then there was the portrait of Eleanor Roosevelt made from a vegetable steamer with a real pearl necklace running inside a kind of track made of cut metal. And a George Washington with a Richard Nixon nose. Over George's head is an American flag made of glass and bottle caps. Written into the image are the words "Slept here, and here, and here."

All of her portraits of famous Americans include clever references to their place in history. Richard Nixon's license plate, for instance, says, "I am not a crook." Benjamin Franklin's portrait includes a metal kite fashioned out of keys. Harriet Tubman is surrounded by a railroad track in reference to the Underground Railroad, and the John F. Kennedy portrait is made out of hole-riddled materials such as a colander and a cheese grater with extra bullet holes.

The centerpiece of the exhibition will be a giant American flag, which I was unable to see as it was laid out on a table and covered with papers and other things. Gallery director Greg Kucera described it as "culled, quilted, mended, basted, stitched and sewn out of hundreds of pieces of found swatches of fabric," adding, "Beecher's obsessiveness is self evident here. Meticulously hand-stitched and measuring over 10 feet in its largest dimension, the flag wavers between savvy indictment and touching homage to American traditions, and manifests the artist's pledge of guarded allegiance."

I think Kucera's use of the term "guarded allegiance" may be the perfect description of Beecher's work with patriotic themes. She exhibits the kind of allegiance shown by patriots who dare to criticize our homeland. Her historic heroes are those embraced by the left, such as Tubman and Kennedy, and her sharpest barbs are directed toward those embraced by the right, epitomized by Nixon. She also seems to identify most strongly with the history of African-Americans. One of the stronger political statements in the show is "Free the Slaves," oil paint on wood and metal. This piece includes a portrait of Abraham Lincoln framed by the presidential seal, with eagle wings coming from behind his head. The brown feathers of the spread eagle's wings are slaves lined up in the hold of a slave ship.

Also showing in May at Greg Kucera is a new series of etchings by Martin Puryear, who is belatedly gaining a national recognition as a sculptor. Puryear has been exhibiting for more than 30 years, but has only recently begun to attract critical attention. Robert Hughes, the acerbic critic for Time magazine, called him America's best sculptor. He has been recognized within the past decade with a Guggenheim Memorial Foundation grant and a MacArthur Foundation grant. He has been included in shows at the Museum of Modern Art in New York and the Hirshhorn Museum in Washington, D.C. And he was the sole representative of the United States to the 1989 Sao Paolo Biennial, where he was awarded the grand prize. Puryear's minimalist and abstract sculpture takes the black experience as its subject matter. The etchings included in this exhibition relate in subject matter and style to his latest sculpture.

## Ric Hall and Ron Schmitt

# Surrealistic Hybrid

*The Weekly Volcano, June 17, 2004*

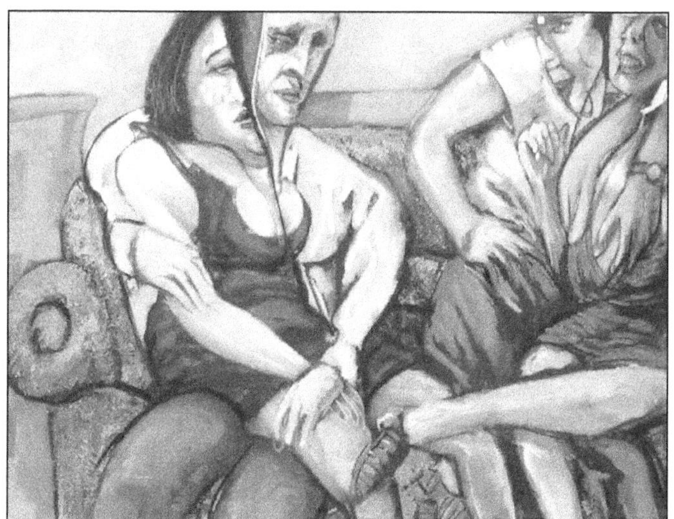

*Ric Hall and Ron Schmitt, "Company" 24"x30," pastel on paper, photo courtesy Brick and Mortar Gallery*

---

Ric Hall and Ron Schmitt work together on pastel paintings of contemporary figures that look like a hybrid of Surrealism and German Expressionism. According to Brick & Mortar Gallery owner Laura Hanan, Hall and Schmitt have been working together for 20 years or longer. And what's more, Hanan tells me that they don't work the way you'd expect collaborative artists to work, with one doing something and then the other responding. Rather, she says, they work simultaneously. I can't imagine what that must be like, but I can imagine that seeing them at work must make for a marvelously entertaining performance.

We can't see them at work, but we can see the end result in an exhibition of 20 of their paintings at Brick & Mortar. The pictures show men and women of a somewhat decadent sort: trailer trash, perhaps, or lovers of country music, young and old folks on the make, folks who hang out in bars and have a lot of apparently unfulfilling sex. They all seem to be worn out, bored and put-upon. They also seem, in quite a few of the paintings, to have suffered facial and bodily harm. Body parts seem to have been torn apart or melted and put back together again.

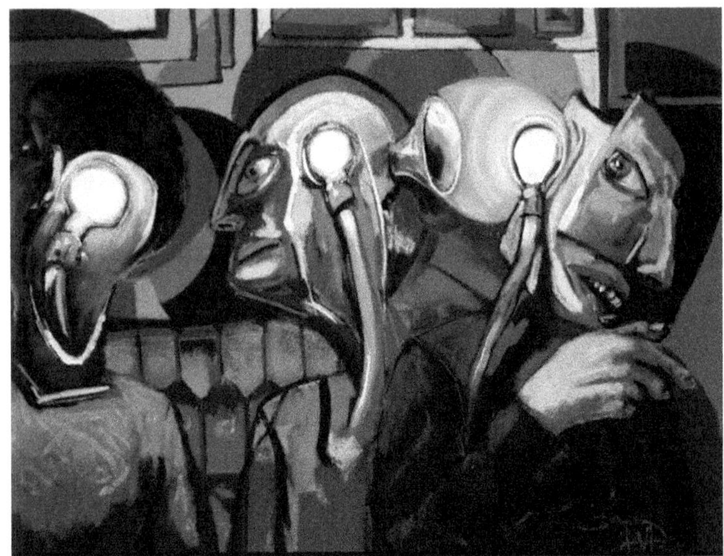

*Ric Hall and Ron Schmitt, "The Edison Project" 24"x18," pastel on paper, photo courtesy of the artist*

One couple, locked in a loveless embrace, appears to have an extra arm. On second glance we see that it's not really an extra arm. It's just in the wrong place. It's hard to tell if it's his or her arm, but it's definitely not protruding from anybody's shoulder. Perhaps it is a prosthetic limb that has been removed and is resting in their mutual lap.

Yet another embracing couple is being torn apart, literally, starting with their heads, which are rendered asunder with a split not unlike an ax blow between their craniums. At least there's no blood.

And there is a man who has thrown his hands over his face and mouth to ward off some evil, as if someone is trying to force-feed him some vile medicine. His hands are a blur of motion with six or seven fingers, and there are marks on his forehead that look like a third hand.

The figures are drawn with confidence. The style is loose, painted with sweeping marks of the pastel. The colors are dark and rich, with warm skin tones vibrant against cool blues.

A very strong influence from Pablo Picasso is in evidence. One picture in particular has a female figure that looks like one of Picasso's portraits of Dora Maar. Other figures — especially emaciated figures and those hovering in doorways — look like figures out of Picasso's rose and blue periods. And there are a few in homage to the master's surrealistic Neo Classical works. A prime example is one in which drawers open out of the body of a heavyset nude. The drawers coming out of the figure are reminiscent of Salvador Dali, but the figure's foot undoubtedly belongs to one of Picasso's gargantuan women.

These paintings are filled with sneaky little surprises that will reveal themselves one after the other if you take the time to really look at them.

While at the gallery, I suggest that you wander back to the wine bar where you will see a number of Hanan's abstract paintings and another group of abstract paintings by Marty Fehl. Fehl's triptychs in oil on board are particularly strong. The industrial-look paint is applied in thick layers of clear color, and they are framed with perforated metal strips that give them the look of sculpted filmstrips. Normally I abhor unusual framing devices, but in this instance the frames become an integral part of the painting, and they are very effective.

There is also a monumental mural above the bar that is worth taking a look at. It was painted by Fehl and Hanan in unintended acknowledgement of Hall and Schmitt's spirit of collaboration.

*The Weekly Volcano, Nov. 22, 2007*

It's as if these guys are co-joined twins with a single brain between them.

Their paintings are figurative and surrealistic with echoes of Picasso and of German Expressionists such as Otto Dix and Max Beckman (one painting titled "Beckman's Legacy" is an obvious homage to the latter). These are dark and disturbing paintings. Or they may be seen as humorous in a twisted sort of way, depending on how warped your sense of humor may be. Although their oeuvre covers the entire range of humanity, from sports to music to family life and more, their show at Mat Hat Tea Company focuses mostly on nightlife and on a kind of revelatory autobiography — but whose biography? Hall's or Schmitt's? Could it be that both of them were smothered in childhood by the engulfing love of slovenly aunts? (The painting "Summers With My Aunts" pictures a frightened young boy, just entering puberty, seated between two women wearing yellow bathing suits and pressing against him in a way that looks to be sexually charged and uncomfortable.)

Sex — clearly discomforting or unsatisfying sex —— rears its head in many of Hall and Schmitt's paintings. Take "Grabbing Mother Nature's Bounty" for example. This painting depicts the Adam and Eve story, but in this one the apple tree is not a tree. It is a voluptuous naked woman with sickly, green skin and a zipper down the middle of her body from neck to crotch. Adam and Eve stand on either side of her (Adam naked and Eve wearing a white tank top and fig leaf). Adam reaches a hand into the open zipper front.

Another that packs a sexual wallop without being pornographic is "Inhibitions Discarded," which pictures a woman in a red dress dancing in front of a couple and a single man drinking in a cabana bar. Her dance is masturbatory, and the people watching are clearly discomforted by being made into voyeurs.

These paintings are inventive and beautifully designed with dark, rich colors and an expressive surface quality more akin to acrylic painting than pastel. Like paintings by the French post-Impressionist Georges Rouault with his vibrant colors outlined in heavy black.

One of the most astounding works in the show, which thematically comes out of left field, is "The Edison Project." The meaning is unclear except that it refers to the inventor of the incandescent light bulb. In this painting, light bulbs have been implanted into the heads of dark and menacing men. The dramatic impact is as powerful as an electric shock.

Not so dramatic but interesting for its clever use of perspective is "Toast to the Way Things Were," which shows diners at a table that becomes a road in a painting going off into the distance with a kind of Renee Magritte-like perspectival trickery.

The lighting at Mad Hat is designed for customer comfort, not for viewing art, and Hall and Schmitt's work is anything but comforting. Nevertheless, this work is worth viewing.

Reilly Jensen

## Simple Stories

*Art Access, April 2003*

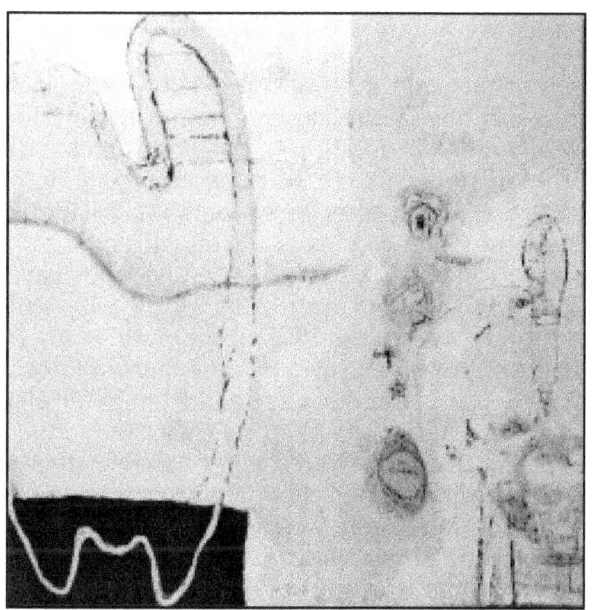

*Reilly Jensen, "when I see you my feet fall off,' 4' x 4' reproduced by permission of the artist*

---

It has been a mere five years since Reilly Jensen turned her attention to painting after 20 years as a graphic artist. But in those five years she has learned lessons about painting that many artists learn only after a lifetime. She seems to own the surface of the canvas, manipulating it with layers of white and gray paint, and with other more brilliant but subtle colors bleeding through; and drawing into the wet surface with a variety of knives, all with a feeling of playful ease and sureness of execution, and without being overly controlled.

Jensen is not yet very well known. Those who are familiar with her work may be surprised at how she has toned down her palette, painting almost exclusively in shades of white, with value contrasts and subtle grays and blues and yellows glowing through a surface that looks like troweled cement. Incised into this surface are quirky and humorous line drawings, and superimposed words painted with liquid black oil paint. Most of the words relate to what Jensen calls the stories behind the paintings. Each painting in the series has its story, and all of her stories are personal (and usually light-hearted and with multiple meanings).

For instance, "shit or get off the pot" is about a friend Jensen says had been struggling with life decisions. She said that when thinking about her friend's struggles it occurred to her that even small decisions can have huge impacts on our lives. This painting comments on anxieties brought on by having to make decisions such as whether or not to take a particular job or go into a particular field of study or enter into a personal relationship. It is painted almost entirely in shades of white, with pink stripes in the left hand corner next to a stack of toilet paper rolls. Layered over the toilet paper rolls — which are drawn, by the way, with lines reminiscent of Andy Warhol's early graphic work — are fields of burning, translucent orange. Scraggly meandering lines that I at first thought were roads in a field as seen from an airplane take up the bottom right quarter of the painting. After long study I realized that this line drawing represented a toilet bowl. Scattered throughout the painting are words related to decision making and risk-taking representing the inner dialogue of someone wracked with indecision. In the upper right hand corner there are two figures poised on an edge. One is diving forward and the other is falling backwards. Finally, a tiny little circle indicating a risk-free zone illustrates just how momentous these decision-making processes can be.

Another example of the types of personal and quirky stories her paintings tell is the painting titled "molar for Scott." Scott is an artist friend who, according to Jensen, collects "a lot of freaky stuff" like skulls and bones and bugs. Her friend Scott has done a lot of paintings with teeth in them, so Jensen decided to paint a large molar for her friend. The molar is drawn in outline with two lines that, as in "shit or get off the pot," looks like a road. This "road" winds from top left past what looks to be plowed fields painted in tones of pink and orange, down across something that looks like either a railroad track or a stream as seen from high in the sky, and finally into a black square at bottom left where one side of the road vanishes and the other becomes a white-on-black line. This painting is loaded with drawings in a rough, graffiti-like style of bones, bugs and skulls. Even the horizontal line I described above as a river or train track turns out, upon closer inspection, to be a line of teeth strung together as in a necklace. It is all very macabre and humorous. There is some marvelously dense and free drawing along with warm colors that peek through heavy white paint with — fittingly in this Halloween scene — a glow reminiscent of lighted candles in a jack-o-lantern.

Jensen spoke of the visual depth in these paintings and how much more difficult is was to create that depth than it had been in her earlier work. Depth came naturally in the earlier works, she said, because of value and hue contrasts that are lacking in the newer works. But depth is an important aspect of these paintings — not illusory depth as in naturalistic landscape, but the kind of shallow depth one sees in a collage where one image is laid over another and then partially torn away to reveal underlying images. There is also an interesting kind of peek-a-boo interplay of lines that at one point appear to be on the surface and another point appear to be behind it.

Another important aspect to her paintings is the asymmetrical placement of forms on the surface. She scatters words and images across the surface in groupings that are tenuously logical and barely in balance. The one exception to her seemingly random use of depth and balance is a painting titled "when i see you my feet fall off." This is a classically balanced painting. Dead center at the top of the painting hangs a pair of legs with no feet. Below that and disconnected are the two feet that have fallen off, feet and pants forming a triangle. The logic and clarity of balance in this painting is augmented by an equally logical placement of objects on two planes. There is underpainting that is clearly on one plane and overpainting that is just as clearly on another plane. None of the other paintings in this series have this kind of logical structure.

There is a playful quality to all of these paintings that Jensen attributes to the influence of California artist Squeak Carnwath, who she said taught her that paintings don't have to be about important subjects. Another influence Seattleites may more easily recognize is Larry Bemm, whose paintings are also very playful and who uses a similar palette. Well known for his shows at Bryan Ohno, Ballard/Fetherston and Linda Cannon galleries, Bemm was compared to Clyfford Still by critic Mathew Kangas, "but with a great deal more informality suggestive of improvised drawing."[1] It is the open field on their canvases, with not quite random placement of objects, along with that informal drawing, that Bemm and Jensen have in common. But Jensen's drawing is more facile, with a feathery touch that reminds me of Arshile Gorky. And I detect in her paintings a more serious intent hidden beneath a playful surface.

1 - review in Art in America, November 2001

Fay Jones and Gaylen Hansen

## Cowboys and Egyptians

*The Weekly Volcano, May 29, 2003*

Walking into the spacious Bill and Bobby Street Gallery in the new Tacoma Art Museum, one is immediately assailed by a painting too large and too audacious to be ignored. Dominating a 10-foot wall section, "Now and Then (The Guide, The Builder, and The Transfer Man)," acrylic, sumi and collage on paper, by Seattle artist Fay Jones, is almost a slap in the face with a dead fish to unwary museum-goers. Looking like a badly drawn cartoon strip from the 1930s on what appears to be three, seven-by-three-foot rolls of butcher paper, "Now and Then" is an assemblage of seemingly unrelated images. There is a Muslim woman with a black monkey perched on or near her shoulder. She holds a cat statue in her third hand. A disembodied head floats in a green sky. There is a man prostrated in prayer behind a red palm tree, and another man surrounded by crickets.

If, after being assaulted by this monstrosity, you are forced to avert your gaze, you naturally look to the left, only to be assaulted by another comical monstrosity, Gaylen Hansen's 60-by-72-inch oil painting, "Man Riding Through Snakes." A cowboy sporting a scraggly beard and a bright red neckerchief rides through a desert surrounded by giant rattlesnakes. Like Jones' painting, this one is big, sloppy and cartoon-like. (Remember my earlier essay, "Seattle Grunge Art"? These are prime examples.)

So what is going on here? Why are such strange and amateurish-looking paintings being presented as major pieces of the opening exhibitions at the new Tacoma Art Museum? Why not something more sedate? More in keeping with the good taste one expects of a major museum? Well, maybe it has to do with the stature of Jones and Hansen, two of the most respected contemporary artists in Washington. Or maybe it has to do with the general funkiness of a region of the country that worships Jimi Hendrix and promotes geoducks as a delicacy.

Jones has been a fixture on the Seattle art scene since the early '70s. Her drawings and paintings and collages are marked by a loose and direct style. Her narrative content is like the poetry of e.e. cummings and Kenneth Patchin — evocative and humorous, usually touching on greater truths, and always presenting more questions than answers. Her drawing style centers on figures delineated by a broken contour with a minimum of details, and filled in by washes of thin color. The size and placement of images in relation to one another always depends on Jones' personal hierarchy, never on anything so mundane as reality or perspective.

The most telling thing about a Fay Jones painting is the incomplete narrative. She always implies a story or indicates possible relationships, but never spells them out. In "Now and Then" she gives hints that the three-panel narrative tells a story about a guide who leads tourists through the ruins of ancient Egypt, thus commenting on the then and now of the title. But most of the story is left to the viewer's imagination.

Hansen, from Eastern Washington, paints tall tales full of fish and bugs and snakes — and a Don Quixote-like character named the Kernal. Hansen's predator animals are usually gigantic, but they never scare the Kernal. In "Man Riding Through Snakes," he seems completely oblivious to the rattlers that are big enough to swallow him whole. Hansen doesn't hint at stories the way Jones does. He simply presents absurdly comical situations and characters and lets them stand on their own. And he does it with a thick, lush painting style that's as rich as icing on a cake.

Jones and Hansen are two of many Northwest artists featured in "Building Tradition: Gifts in Honor of the Northwest Art Collection." This is the first part of a three-part exhibition honoring hundreds of Northwest artists. In addition to Jones and Hansen, the current show features works by photographers Imogene Cunningham and Mary Randlett, and many other regional artists.

## Paul and Dante Marioni

# Rocking glass

*The Weekly Volcano, Feb. 21, 2008*

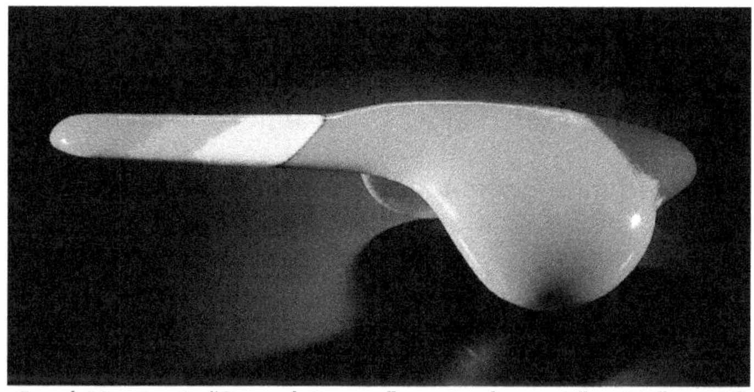

*Paul Marioni, "Speed Racer" cast glass, 5" x 19" x 10"*

Father and son glass artists Paul (father) and Dante (son) Marioni are showing together for only the second time anywhere at William Traver Gallery in Tacoma. Going against all reasonable expectations, it is the father whose work displays a more youthful, impish and edgy attitude, while the younger Marioni is immersed in the mastery of traditional techniques — not that they're not both excellent craftsmen.

Dante makes elegant vessels in blown and cast glass that are sleek and colorful. He has two contrasting bodies of work in this show, a series of leaf and acorn shaped vessels using the reticello technique and tall vases in brilliant colors with strange handles in starkly contrasting colors. They are all quite beautiful.

And I might as well confess right now that I am not particularly enamored of glass art. I'm rather sick of the proliferation of glass in the Northwest. But Marioni's vases are outstanding. His vases have curvilinear handles in odd colors, often multiple handles that crawl up the sides of the vases like spiders or trellises or Shiva arms, and typically the rims and bases are the same color as the handles. One of his more striking pieces is "Red with Yellow Vessel Display," which is a wooden display case for 12 red vessels with orange handles, each differently shaped but identical in height. They look like strange medieval chess figures or an army of alien creatures.

The reticello technique creates diamond-shaped patterns by twisting and fusing together two cane cups in a manner that traps air and thus creates a little air bubble inside each diamond. There are about half a dozen reticello vessels in this show, all in clear glass with the crossing diamond lines in black and white creating moiré patterns that move with the viewer. I particularly liked the pair sitting in front of the window with the cone of the Museum of Glass visible behind them, because the cone has an identical surface pattern. I asked. That wasn't planned. But what a terrific coincidence.

Paul Marioni's works are more sculptural. They are all part of a series called "I Am in Motion," and each of his sculptures is perfectly balanced to rock when touched by hand. Most are saddle- or turtle shell-shaped, but in many of them the overall saddle shape is manipulated to take the form of human bodies or faces. The bodies embrace, and you'd have to be blind not to see the sexual innuendo or the references to yin-yang and infinity symbols.

"Speed Racer" is shaped like a turtle with a long neck and head sticking out from its shell, and I can't help but see it as a small version of the rocking-phallus murder weapon in "A Clockwork Orange" in brilliant bands of red, orange, yellow and blue. It is comical and quite beautiful.

"The Calculated Lie" is a figure eight or infinity symbol in clear glass that will keep rocking for up to 20 minutes, I'm told, at the merest touch (it never stopped rocking when I was in the gallery).

Two of my favorites are "Trophy," cast glass and enamel, and "Black Trophy," cast glass, enamel and gold leaf. I like the simplicity of these and the painterly quality of the surface decoration. Plus, I like that they are less gimmicky than the more figurative pieces.

Any one of his rocking sculptures would make wonderful conversation pieces if you had them on your coffee table, but these are pretty big-name artists and not many people can afford them. I was told that Elton John just bought one. If I were Elton John, I'd buy one, too.

Barlow Palminteri

## New kid on the block

*The Weekly Volcano, May 27, 2004*

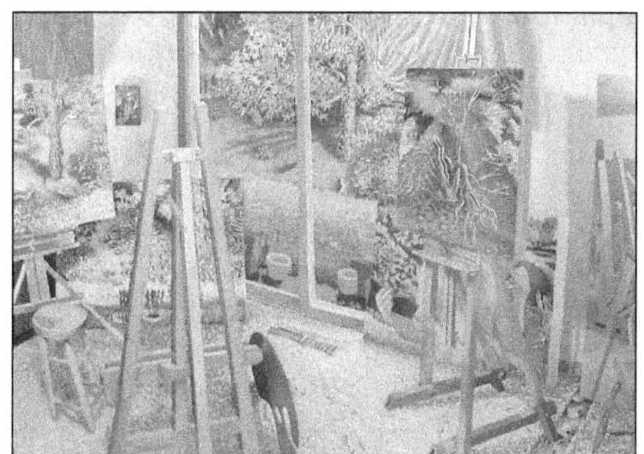

*Barlow Palminteri, "Easel" acrylic on canvas, 74½"x106½," reproduced by permission of the artist*

I had never heard of Barlow Palminteri until I got an e-mail urging me to see his show at the SideDoor Studio in Olympia. Apparently nobody else has heard of him either. Gallery director Lori Vermillion said Barlow "paints for himself" and has never before shown his work.

Wow! Here is a mature artist, well schooled in all the nuances of color and composition, who has spent what must have been years perfecting his art in private, and suddenly he bursts upon the public scene with about a dozen large scale paintings that simply knock your socks off.

Palminteri's paintings are intricately designed, complex and colorful. They explore a single theme with a variety of shapes and colors all held in check within a grid and unified by hue and value choices. And the paint is applied with confidence.

What do I mean by "applied with confidence?" I mean that you can see that there was no hesitance. There is a consistency to his paint application, and little or no evidence of adjusting or correcting in process. He juxtaposes smooth areas of flat color with no blending alongside brushstrokes that are laid down in short Impressionist-like strokes (Imagine van Gogh with a softer stroke).

There are eleven paintings in the show. Half of them are large paintings, approximately 8 to 10 feet in width. The rest measure approximately 20-by-30 inches. Displayed in order of execution, each painting is a variation on the painting that came before it. I will explain:

First he painted a picture of himself painting in his studio. Then he did a painting of this painting propped on an easel with other paintings in the studio, and then a painting of the same painting now shoved against the wall and almost hidden by other paintings, and then a mirror image of himself painting the painting of the painting — and so forth throughout the series.

His colors are so bright that they almost hurt the eye. Harsh hot oranges, buttery yellows and acid yellow-greens predominate — sunwashed colors that are held in check by carefully placed muted areas where these same colors are dulled down with soft gray tones.

Although each painting is of the same subject, but with the objects in different configurations, Palminteri differentiates them with titles based on whatever item is most prominent: chairs, easel, mirror, etc.

In "Chairs," two empty chairs sit facing each other. On the left is a brown wooden chair. Behind it are brown and gray paintings on easels, all in muted colors. On the right is an orange chair in front of orange and yellow and blue paintings, all in intense colors. The whole composition is made up of shifting planes of dull and intense colors.

"Mirror" places a full-figured self-portrait seen in a mirror in the middle of the canvas. Peeking out on either side are parts of easels, paintings, chairs and plants. Strategically, edges of objects outside the mirror image line up with similar objects (mostly of the same color) within the mirror so that it becomes a hide-and-seek game of inside and outside.

Inside and outside configurations play a large role in "Easels." In this one, the original self portrait is hidden behind a painting of plants on an easel in front of a sliding glass door that opens onto a patio filled with more plants, and off to the side there are more paintings of plants. Even the brushstrokes on the carpeted floor mirror the undulating forms of fronds and grass outside and in the paintings.

These are excellent paintings in a tradition handed down from Pierre Bonnard and Henri Matisse.

Dave Wegener

## Word games in paint

*The Weekly Volcano, March 20, 2003*

Dave Wegener's painting exhibition at Childhood's End Gallery in Olympia is based on a highly intelligent concept. It is also very attractive, and there's not much more you can ask of art than that. The only gripe I have with Wegener's show — and it's a minor gripe — is that there is a kind of slick look to the paintings. The paint has been allowed to drip and run, and the surface is roughly textured, all of which would normally indicate a certain amount of spontaneity and/or struggle. And yet every brushstroke looks to have been preconceived and carefully placed, giving the paintings a contrived look, which is heightened by the high-gloss finish.

Ah! But they're such intelligent paintings! And there is so much to see and think about in Wegener's simple combinations of shapes and letters. The show is called "*Admonitvm*," Latin for admonition. There are ten paintings in the show. Each painting is a metaphor for a theme, and each represents a letter. Read left to right, the paintings make up the Latin word *Vitabrevis*, which is an admonition to be mindful of the brevity of life. There is a wall text mounted in the gallery to explain this rather complicated concept. Without it, no one would be able to figure it out; but by using visual and verbal clues provided in the paintings and in the wall text, the whole group of ten paintings becomes an educational puzzle.

Each painting is a collage of either newsprint or pictures and raised, Roman letters spelling out Latin words, over which the artist has painted simple shapes in broad strokes of semi-transparent paint.

The first painting to be seen is actually the last painting in the series, "*Scrvtor*," or the letter S, meaning "Consider what you lose with each thing you gain." According to the Latin dictionary I used, *Scrvtor* means "search/probe/examine carefully/thoroughly." But I can't help but see similarities to the word scribe, which means a writer. And what does the modern writer write with? A mouse. This painting is a picture of two computer mice painted black and white to form a yin-yang symbol. The edges between the black and white also create the letter S. On the black mouse is a dollar sign and on the white mouse a black heart. Also, very faintly seen beneath layers of transparent paint are collaged pictures of happy children's faces. Between the yin-yang, the black and white, the symbol for money and the black heart, this painting is loaded with symbolism. Each viewer can probably find his or her own meanings, but it would be hard to ignore the implications of a struggle between good and evil and the hope offered in the laughing children's faces (especially in view of the admonition to reflect on the brevity of life).

I may be reading more into the paintings than was intended, but I think the artists would like for viewers to find their own meanings in them. The only other comment I would like to make is that Wegener has obviously been influenced by Jim Dine and Jasper Johns, who are pretty good role models for a contemporary painter.

Marita Dingus

# 400 African Men and Buddha

*The Weekly Volcano, May 13, 2004*

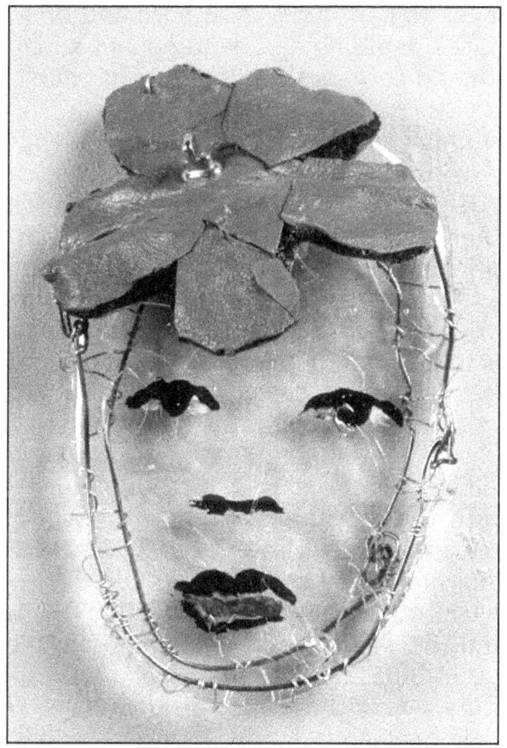

*Marita Dingus, "See through Me #2" glass and mixed media, 11"x7½"x3," photo by Richard Nicol, courtesy Francine Seders Gallery*

---

Marita Dingus. Don't you just love that name? I certainly do, and I love her art, too. Dingus is revered for quirky masks and figures made of recycled materials that — while addressing such serious topics as slavery and poverty — nevertheless manage to be whimsical and cheerful.

Now Dingus adds glass to her repertoire of materials. "Glass is a new medium for me," she explained. "I wanted to contrast the shiny, smooth transparency and permanence of glass with the softness, flexibility and light weight of fabric, with some found objects thrown in."

A short time ago she did a five-day residency at the Museum of Glass, during which time she produced sixty faces in painted and cast glass. That's sixty in five days. She's nothing if not prolific. And then she went back to her studio in Auburn and built funky bodies to go with her faces, molding and bending and stitching them out of wire and cloth and cork and whatnot in what must have been a hurricane of activity.

How anybody can work so fast boggles the mind. She must create art the way Jack Kerouac wrote — no editing, no rewrites, no agonizing over getting the words just right. (Digression: Truman Capote said of Kerouac "That's not writing. That's typing.") Back to Dingus: Normally one might expect such an outpouring to result in an undisciplined hodgepodge of aesthetic vomit, but in Dingus's art it seems to work, because each piece is so personal and heartfelt. Plus, she seems to have an unerring sense of what goes with what, which means that maybe she never has to fine-tune her work. Either that or she hasn't slept in five months.

Included in her exhibition at the Museum of Glass are the aforementioned sixty glass and mixed media figures plus a number of familiar pieces from previous exhibitions, most notably at Francine Seders Gallery in Seattle.

One of her most famous pieces is "Buddha as an African Enslaved." On a trip to China she saw a Buddha that was as large as a skyscraper, and she was moved to make her own version in cloth. The result was a 63-foot tall figure that could be displayed only when turned on its side and wrapped around walls. So large that the figure was visually pressed between floor and ceiling, it reminded her of pictures of slaves stuffed into compartments on slave ships. It has an emaciated body made from woven bits of cloth, a huge blue-black African face, and hands flattened into glove-like monstrosities. In previous shows it has stretched around corners. This is the first time it has ever been shown on a wall big enough to hold the whole thing.

Two other wall-size pieces are "400 African Men" and "200 African Woman." These were inspired by a visit to slave holding cells in Africa. The tiny headless dolls are arranged in rectangular bars (the men) and in concentric ovals (the women). They are headless because to the slave traders heads and minds did not count, only bodies. The arrangements also reflect on the way slaves were herded like cattle and jammed into tiny spaces. Seen as overall patterns of repetitive forms, these works can be mesmerizing, and it is equally fascinating to study the immense variety of form and material within the individual doll bodies.

The sixty glass faces made during her residency are all relatively flat in clear glass with features painted on. In some, the painting is on the glass surface; in others, clear glass is layered over the painted surface. Some are presented as stand-alone faces that either hang on the wall or are set on stands like decorative plates, and many are given life-size bodies made of scrap cloth and wire. Cast shadows and light reflecting off the glass, and the many metallic wires and threads throughout the pieces, create a shimmering wonderland effect throughout the whole gallery.

Chauney Peck

# Evolution

*The evolution of a young artist, Chauney Peck, is traced through four reviews in the Weekly Volcano spanning the years 2003 to 2007*

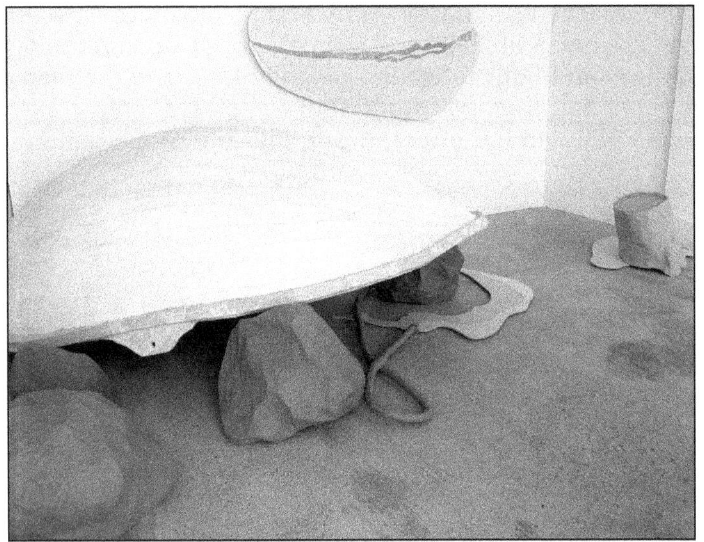

*Chaney Peck, "Surrender" painted wood, various dimensions, photo courtesy of the artist.*

---

## Sexy fish

*April 2003*

Olympia's latest art venue is The Mark, a fine restaurant downtown. Currently showing is an exhibition with the provocative title "The Last Desires of Fish: New Drawings by Chauney Peck."

It is hard for me to reviews these drawings objectively, because they remind me too much of an artsy-craftsy kind of schlock art that I detest: prints made by inking fish and pressing them against paper. Very corny stuff. But Peck's drawings are not corny at all. Well, maybe just a little bit (I warned you it was hard for me to be objective).

Inside The Mark there are two dining areas, and each area features a different grouping of Peck's art. A group of six works on paper is shown in the front dining lounge, and a group of three larger works on canvas fills the back dining room. The only significant differences in the two groups are size and media. Each drawing depicts a highly abstracted fish, along with a spattering of marks, some of which are obviously derived from seaweed or algae or other aquatic life, and some of which stand alone as graphic elements with no outside reference. Images are widely dispersed on a neutral background. Placement seems random, but there are discernable patterns. It all seems to belong to a kind of chaos theory of design that is probably more intuitive than contrived.

The paint application is mostly thin and the drawing is sketchy and spontaneous, with an apparently purposeful unfinished look. I found that I was drawn to them as if to a puzzle, because, beyond recognizing the fish in each, the interesting thing was seeing how her apparently random marks fit together: here a staccato line, there a clump of something like balls of string, over there a blob of blended graphite, and down there a thin wash of runny paint. But one color may reflect another and one shape may lead the eye to another, and the viewer's eye keeps moving over the whole. The order within the chaos emerges slowly.

There is a kind of sweetness to many of these, and I, personally, am put off by that. But, on the other hand, that very sweetness makes those that are not so sweet seem very bold. For instance, in some of the drawings the fish are upside-down, and everyone knows that upside-down fish are dead fish. And in some there are very rough lines on top of the fish that look like they were drawn with a bold and rapid movement, and these create a sense of violence. These fish have been cut and perhaps tangled in a fishing line or net. It kind of makes me hope they don't serve fish at The Mark.

## The eatery queen

*March 2004*

Chauney Peck may be on her way to becoming the queen of eatery art. A year ago she showed at The Mark, a restaurant in Olympia. Now she is showing a new body of work at Batdorf and Bronson, a coffee roaster. In each of these exhibits, she displayed a series of paintings based on a specific theme — fish at The Mark and now birds at Batdorf. Is this the beginning of a trend? Will we next see dogs at Tully's and insects at the Kickstand?

I hope so. Maybe she could even extend her artistic exploration into different approaches to media for each series as she has here (her fish painting were works on paper and canvas; the bird paintings on vinyl and paper).

There are eight paintings in her current show, each modest in size, which would have been necessary because of the limited space. Each painting is acrylic on layered sheets of vinyl and paper. She uses a combination of opaque and transparent paints to maximize the effect of seeing through layer after layer, and her transparencies vary from almost invisible through degrees of translucency, and from sketchy and open marks to dense puddles of solid paint — all of which serves to unify the different levels in intriguing ways. By this I mean that the viewers can easily grasp that they are looking through layers of transparencies but cannot always tell which images are on top and which are underneath. There are also shapes that appear to have been painted on the underside of the glass that covers the paintings, although this could be an illusion. This is highly effective, but the effect falls apart in one or two paintings where shapes painted in a solid color are too obviously painted on the top layer and thus stand out like lipstick on a white shirt, and destroy the unity of the painting.

Peck paints her images with sketchy, loopy and staccato marks that are like little bursts of controlled energy in seemingly random placement. Some of her bird images are drawn with rhythmical strokes and well-defined contours and others are barely hinted at with scratchy and runny marks. Some are easily recognizable as birds, while others are seen as parts — a beak here, a wing there, a claw somewhere else. Flowing in and around these are clumps of paint that do not necessarily define anything but convey the feel of feathers, beaks, twigs, clouds and trees.

A common tendency seen in these paintings is to group her images in loosely circular patterns around the edges of the surface, leaving an open white emptiness in the middle. The ones in which she employs this device are more successful than the ones in which she places images closer to the center. That open center with forms swirling around nearer the edges creates an exciting feel of energy. Similarly, I find that the paintings in which her forms are less defined are more exciting and better unified than the ones in which the forms are more easily read as subject matter. A squiggle of paint suggesting a tangle of bush involves the viewer in a much more lasting way than does a bird drawn with careful contour lines.

## Ride the Art

*May 4th 2006*

Chauney Peck's installation at Icebox Contemporary Art brings to mind The Beatles' "Lucy in the Sky with Diamonds." I pictured myself in a boat on a river with tangerine trees and marmalade skies. Her art is not an illustration of Lennon's lyrics, nor are there the psychedelic colors the song describes. The boat isn't even on the river; it's turned upside-down on the rocks and looks like nothing so much as an old turtle's shell. Nevertheless, it evokes that image. That's what art does when art does what it does. It transports the viewer. It evokes memory and reverie.

I close my eyes and look again, and now it looks like a theatrical set. I expect at any moment to see actors come out costumed as birds and squirrels and fish and fishermen. A children's play filled with magic.

Peck's installation is small and unpretentious, and has a bulky, cartoon look. The aforementioned boat is made of paper maché and is painted a dull brown. It rests on massive gray rocks (also paper maché) as if dragged out of the water and set that way to keep the rain out. Underneath the boat is a length of rope (not real rope, but more painted paper maché), and surrounding it are cut-out wooden shapes to represent flowing water, painted tree stumps and more rocks. On the walls are billowy clouds made from cut and assembled sheets of wood. Color changes in the clouds are formed by varying wood grains. One of the clouds looks like a giant hamburger, or perhaps an oyster in its shell. Another one is shaped like some kind of fanciful animal, or perhaps a childlike silhouette of an island.

Everything is painted in dull, chalky tones of brown, green and gray, colors in keeping with the walls and unfinished concrete floor. Forms and colors fit so well with the interior of the building, in fact, that I had to ask if something had been done to the floors and if a kind of concrete rail against one wall was part of the installation. (It's not.)

Technically, Peck's installation is well made. Details are minimized. It has the look of something made in a 10th grade art class or, in keeping with the look of a theatrical set, something designed to be seen from a distance.

The artist says this piece was inspired by a dream she had last spring. "Mom, Dad and I were in a rowboat fending off tree stumps and barnacle encrusted rocks with our hands. We slowly meandered through the shallow salt water. Mom lost her wedding band and we searched for it in the muck. We landed on an island. The boat washed away. We crawled on hands and knees through thick woods. Dad was hungry."

Chauney Peck is a young artist on the go. I have admired her paintings since first seeing a piece in one of the final shows at Commencement Art Gallery. Since then she has been amazingly prolific and has had more gallery showings than most artists right out of school. She paints floral and animal forms (most commonly aquatic) with energetic brushstrokes and a staccato drawing style reminiscent of Cy Twombly. The current work is the first three-dimensional work I've seen from her. It's interesting stuff. I'd like to see where she might go with this new direction. But I hope she doesn't give up painting. This work does not have the verve of her paintings, but it does share with her paintings a fine sense of placement and weight distribution. In the paintings, objects float in shallow space; in this sculptural work there is a similar feel of not-quite random placement of objects with space all around.

## Urban debris

*Nov. 1, 2007*

I've been following the evolution of Chauney Peck since the late '90s when she showed up in a group show at the old Commencement Art Gallery.

Back then she was doing paintings that were expressive, spatially open and gestural. Then she evolved into a sculptor of large, painted wood constructions that looked something like giant jigsaw puzzles — a typical example being the big, cartoon-like boat she displayed at Ice Box Gallery last year. That boat and similar constructions presented an interesting twist on tradition: Paintings in the Renaissance tradition used perspective to create an illusion of three-dimensional space on a flat surface; in her painted constructions, Peck created an illusion of flat space in three-dimensional objects.

Her vinyl paintings on paper at The Helm bring together many of the visual concerns dealt with in her earlier works. She paints clumps or piles of urban debris — cast-off clothing, toys, furniture; the accumulated crap of a wasteful, consumer society. Everything is piled together into a single shape surrounded by white space. Her compositions are highly structured and architectural in the way of Cezanne when he broke the forms of nature down to their essential geometric shapes. Her flat, unmodulated colors and flowing lines remind me a lot of the artwork of Jacob Lawrence.

As a typical example, "Cerrado" pictures a pile of furniture with blue cloths (perhaps referring to the blue tarps that were so prominent in New Orleans after Katrina), a light bulb reminiscent of Picasso's eye-bulb in "Guernica," a red bucket and overturned patio furniture. The whole structure is a single form that has a dramatic thrust from a clutter of objects lower right to the light bulb upper left. The colors are bright and flat, and the whole assemblage of objects is held together by careful placement and by the zippy white lines that tie the parts together.

Showing with Peck is Whiting Tennis, whose paintings and sculptures deal with many of the same subjects and are similar in style. The two are so similar in both style and outlook that it would be easy to assume that everything in the gallery was created by the same artist. They are a perfect match.

In fact, I thought Tennis' "Blue Hamburger" was by Peck until I read the inventory sheet. "Blue Hamburger" is a painting in acrylic and collage on canvas of a third world tent city, a cluttered amalgamation of thrown-together shacks and tents constructed of discarded materials. As in Peck's paintings, all of the objects are clumped together to form a single organic shape on a white background. The differences are to be found in Tennis' use of simulated wood-grain texture and his limited palette. Peck's primary colors give way to mostly whites and grays in Tennis. But both employ the ubiquitous blue tarps. Tennis' work is also grittier. Life seems harsher in his world. Whereas Peck also depicts poverty amidst plenty, she presents it in a playful style reminiscent of Japanese animé.

The most powerful works by Tennis are two rather large sculptures: "The New Green" (wood, paint and Visqueen) and "Boogeyman" (plywood and hot metal tar). "The New Green" is an enigmatic structure that looks something like a strangely-shaped dog house painted a sickly, milky green. It is a self-contained structure that is compelling because of its mystery. What could its function possibly be? "Boogeyman" is identical in shape but completely covered in shiny black tar to give it the menacing look of some kind of military apparatus or a mechanized Darth Vader mask.

This is truly an excellent show.

## Holly Senn
# Narrative Redux

*The Weekly Volcano, December 2006*

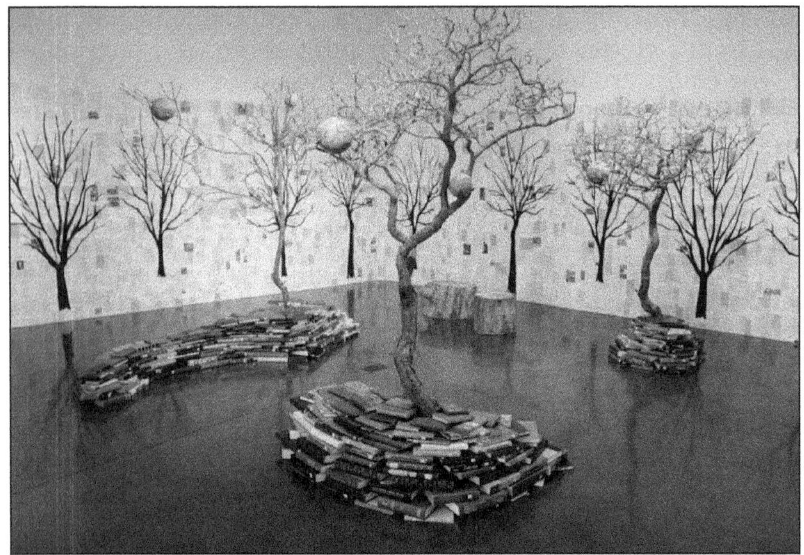

*Holly Senn, "Enchanted Forest of the Mind" installation at The Gallery at Tacoma Community College December 2006. Photo by Duncan Price.*

---

Over the past three years, I have watched Holly Senn gradually and methodically refine her art. Her materials and themes never change, but her statements are becoming clearer and she is fine tuning her use of words, materials and space. Her latest work combines a room-size installation with free-standing sculpture and two-dimensional wall hangings. The show is called Enchanted Forest of the Mind.

Senn defines her work as being about "the lifecycle of ideas." Her materials are discarded books, tree trunks and branches, and printed text. It is crucial to her way of thinking that all the materials she uses have been discarded.

A coherent installation fills the back room of the gallery. It is a forest of constructed trees. Three walls are fully wallpapered with pages from books. Evenly spaced around the walls are starkly naked trees spray painted on the pages with black paint. In the center of the room are two tree stumps and three gnarled trees that stand on islands of books. Giant globe-shaped leaf pods constructed from paper with printed text hang from the branches. The islands of books are carefully arranged with an eye toward the overall shape and the colors and textures of the books. This forest has the contemplative ambiance of a Japanese garden. Viewers are invited to wander through and even sit on the stumps. Sit and think about the beauty of trees and the loss of those that have been cut down to make room for commercial development or to make lumber for building or paper for books — books that nourish our minds but eventually get tossed on the trash heap.

In the middle gallery are two related wall pieces and a few free-standing sculptures. The larger of the two wall pieces consists of three large sheets of cardboard. Tree shapes are cut out of the cardboard and are seen as the glaring white of the wall shining through the negative cut-out shapes to form the image of three trees hung upside-down on the wall. The stark contrast of the white tree limbs is enhanced with black spray paint around the edges, which resonates with the black spray-painted trees in the back gallery. The pieces that were cut out to form the tree shapes are hung on an adjacent wall stacked one on top of another, and also hung upside-down.

The free-standing sculptures consist of leaves or pods made from paper with printed text hung on tree limbs. Most are approximately two-to-three feet in height and stand on standard sculpture pedestals. Most have a blunt and emphatic look with a small number of pods that are, relative to the size of the branches, huge. But one, titled “Narrative Redux” is delicate and lacy. The limbs are thin. Hanging from the branches are tiny tags, each with a single word printed on them. Its base is an old history book. Some of the words printed on the tags are: Cities, Lender, Greeks, Church, Clash and Control.

In the front room stands a massive tree, with a trunk about eight inches in diameter and huge seed pods made from paper with digitized print in type fonts ranging in size from approximately 36 to 78 point. They look like hanging paper lanterns. Like the others, this tree stands on an island of books; unlike the others, these books are randomly scattered. The papered wall behind the tree is painted green.

This is the fifth Holly Senn installation or exhibition I've seen, and it is the most fully realized. My challenge to her now would be to fill a space equal to or larger than the TCC gallery with a single installation in which all the pieces are fully integrated into a visual and thematic whole (as opposed to being a hybrid between installation art and separate art objects).

## Donald Cole

# Shapes that mimic language

*Art Access December 2007*

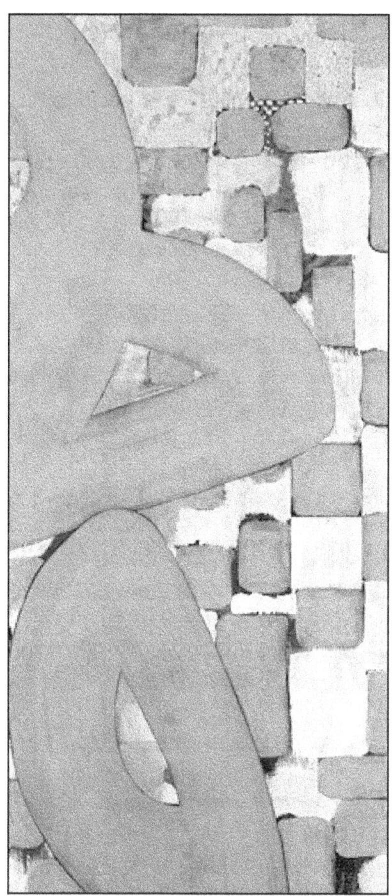

*Donald Cole, "Rupas (Forms)" acrylic on canvas, 54"x24", photo courtesy ArtXchange*

Donald Cole knows a little something about the juxtaposition of abstract shapes on a flat surface. He knows a little something about sunburnt colors and the layering of surfaces in shallow space, and about all the mark-making tools at a painter's disposal, like stippling and scraping and the careful laying on of paint.

At least that's what his paintings look like when viewed on a computer screen. I have not yet had an opportunity to see the paintings in his show at ArtXchange, and reproductions on a Web site can sometimes be deceiving. What appear to be rough surfaces of scraped, gouged and layered paint may not be. A photograph on his Web site of Cole at work looks like he is carefully painting small details with a sable brush on an unstretched canvas that is laid across his bed. (Evidence from other painters confirms how deceiving such appearances can be. Works by Jackson Pollock and Willem de Kooning, for instance, as well some of Gerhardt Richter's abstract paintings, look like they were painted with fast and furious brushstrokes, but films of them at work prove they were much more methodical than the paintings look.)

I suspect that Cole is also more methodical in his painting than a cursory glance at the work indicates, although a gallery news release does speak of his surfaces as being "distressed" and "cracked."

Cole's paintings are 99 percent abstract, and feature fat calligraphic shapes that look like Asian writing or ancient hieroglyphs and other iconic symbols laid on top of rock-like shapes in dull, cool blues and greens over hot reds and burnt oranges, with adjacent deep transparencies in some areas and flat, opaque shapes in others. His surfaces evoke landscapes with winding roads or rivers or frescoes on old, crumbling stone walls. The paintings look to be informed by nature as opposed to being drawn from or imitative of nature. Seldom does recognizable and intentional subject matter appear, but Indian figures show up in some of his paintings — Indians from India, not Native American Indians. And according to the gallery, the squiggly abstract writing is drawn from Asian writing. A press release states: "Cole contrasts the angular forms of Sanskrit with the rounder, gestural forms of Malayalam, the language of Kerala, in south India. In the latest works, the written characters themselves become even more abstract, creating texts of Cole's own design — shapes that mimic language, but whose meanings lie somewhere in the emotive qualities of the paintings themselves."

Originally from New York, where he has shown in such prestigious galleries as 55 Mercer Gallery, French & Co., and the Nancy Hoffman Gallery, Cole now lives on Vashon Island. His current show at ArtXchange is called "Unpredictable Arrivals."

"During the last twenty years my main inspiration has come from extensive travel in Asia where one is bombarded by complex layers of forms and colors and by the many creative expressions of spirituality that pervade Asian life, especially in India," Cole writes in a personal statement on his Web site. "The signs and symbols and the effects of time and weather on the shrines and walls affect the content of my work and balance my formal concerns with human and caring concerns."

The ArtXchange show features 23 recent paintings and one wall-size earlier work, "Rockwall," which is a precursor of many of the more recent paintings.

"Rockwall" looks like a landscape painted in brilliant reds, blues and oranges on a stone wall shot through with white cracks. A dark blue river meanders across the top section separating walls of red and orange rock. Deep red calligraphic marks dance across the surface.

Similar marks, but looking more controlled, show up in many of his later paintings. Dark, hot and vibrant earth tones predominate, and the designs are densely packed. But two of my favorites are cooler in tone and with fewer shapes and less overlay. They are "Rupas (Forms)" and "Citi (Brick)," both of which show a few very simple organic shapes in tones of blue, green and yellow over fields of rock-like rectangles with rounded edges. In both the colors are milky and dull, with everything keyed to a middle value.

Measuring 54 by 24 inches, "Rupas" is a tall, thin painting with two large calligraphic letters that look almost like human legs. The upper "leg" drapes down from the top edge of the canvas and forms a triangle that barely kisses the edge of the lower "leg," which looks like a raised knee. The top one is a dull, yellow-green and the bottom one the same green with hints of ochre. The yellow and green rectangles in the background are jammed together like pieces of a crude, hand-made rock puzzle. "Citi," which is the same size and dimensions, has a pair of oval shapes in dull blue and violet jammed against the left edge of the canvas and to the right a squiggle of the same dull blue that looks like the bend of a river going nowhere or a coiled and striking snake.

"Chaun (To Transmit)" has blue and ochre letters dancing on a dark brick red background. Two of the letters look like Keith Haring figures boxing.

One of the few paintings with recognizable figures is "Echo," which shows a dark, reddish-brown figure walking past what appears to be stone buildings with writing on the walls. The figure is comical looking, with spiked hair (or a crown) and is carrying a sword. There are marvelously deep transparencies in this painting.

Two others with obvious figures are "Shifafa (Lyric Energy)" and "Essential Nature," both of which picture seated Indian gods (most likely Siva, the god of destruction) with overlapping transparent fields of writing. I think these suffer from being too literal, and that the more abstract images and the simpler designs are much stronger.

*Author's note: I visited the gallery after this review was published, and the paintings were much more impressive than the Web site images had suggested.*

# What's it all about?

Is the act of making art a worthwhile thing? Despite the proliferation of new forms — installation, conceptual, environmental, performance, video, etc. — the most frequently seen art today remains what it has always been, objects made for aesthetic appreciation. So the question remains, are the objects we place on pedestals and hang on our walls for decoration worthy of the adoration that has been heaped upon them? And what of the new art forms? Are they merely entertainment, no more or less worthy of our attention than, say, open mic night at your local comedy club?

What about the exorbitant price tags on some works of art — $142.7 million for a Pollock, $140.2 million for a de Kooning, $129.7 million for van Gogh's portrait of Dr. Gachet? On a more practical level, is the watercolor by a little-known artist in the gallery down the street worth its $150 price tag? And what of earth art such as Robert Smithson's "Spiral Jetty," which no one can own, or temporary installations such as Jean-Claude and Christo's gates in Central Park, which now exist only in photographs and in memory? How do you place a value on such as these?

How do we determine the worth of art in terms of its emotional or intellectual reward or the satisfaction we derive from hanging a painting over our couch?

What about the value of art to society? With a few exceptions, a work of art does not feed the hungry or shelter the homeless or put a stop to war. It has been said that art can foster love and understanding among people, and I believe that is true. I also believe that in ways too ephemeral to understand, art can promote peace and harmony, can help us see our world and our fellow human beings with more compassion, and can stretch our minds in ways not possible with any other means of entertainment or communication.

The painter Henri Matisse said that a good painting was like a comfortable chair, but I believe art should offer something far beyond mere comfort. Art can be transformative, transcendental or exalting. It can open up new vistas, new ideas, new ways of seeing; it can help people from various social and political backgrounds better understand one another, and it can challenge us to reexamine our beliefs.

In days gone by art served religious, historical and educational purposes. In the past century there was much talk of art for art's sake; the purposes of art were aesthetic. Over the past half century, the means and purposes of art have expanded to include new forms and approaches, and we have been challenged to rethink our ideas about art.

Shortly after I published the first version of this book I took part in a discussion group in which a small number of artists talked about Suzi Gablik's book *The Reenchantment of Art*. In this book, Gablik made the case for a new paradigm for art that "attempts to engage the whole being — not just the intellect but the emotional, psychological, ethical and spiritual parts of us as well." She spoke of art as being no longer a question of style or content but of social and environmental responsibility.

Among examples in Gablik's book of art that answered the call to environmental and social responsibility were shopping carts for homeless people created by Krzystof Wodiczko and Dominique Mazeaud's project to clean up litter in the Rio Grande River. While some people may applaud such projects for their social responsibility, they may question whether or not they are art.

Just as John Cage called for artists to "efface the boundaries between art and life," in a series of lectures at Black Mountain College as early as 1952, Gablik called for artists to efface the boundaries between art and social or political activism. Growing out of Cage's lectures were happenings and performance art — new art forms and new paradigms that exploded previous artistic boundaries and were the precursors to art events (for lack of a better term) such as Mazeud's Rio Grande project.

In this book's title essay I quoted Cage and Marshall McLuhan: "...is a truck in a music school more musical than a truck passing by in the street?" (Cage), and "Art is anything you can get away with" (McLuhan). The post-modernist, pluralistic and anything-goes implications of such quotes no longer seem radical. Truly anything goes today. This is the wide-open world of art that I called for in my graduate thesis in 1970. The subtitle of my thesis, "an alternative to the frame-pedestal aesthetic," is essentially what Cage called for when he exhorted artists to "efface the boundaries between art and life," and I think it is essentially what Gablik describes as the new paradigm.

Art today can excite, stimulate, enlighten and challenge viewers as never before. I applaud the broadening of art and the tremendous variety of artistic expression it has spawned. But there are downsides. The post-modernist zeitgeist has opened the floodgates not only to new forms, but to a torrent of mediocrity. While the "avant-garde" would have us believe there is longer a place for art as a beautiful object, mainstream galleries present the public with what seems to be a never-ending stream of warmed-over Cubism and Impressionism and Surrealism, and even realism in the Pre-Raphaelite style, not to mention "modernistic" landscapes that are minimalist with softly blurred horizon lines, and coy studio nudes, and sweet abstractions that safely avoid any jarring edges. (They might as well show big-eyed kids and poker playing dogs.) And "cutting edge" galleries show installations and conceptual pieces that are either too difficult to understand or, if we look deeply enough, turn out to be meaningless. Or they show art that is politically edgy or sexual in ways that go far beyond what many consider in good taste. It becomes harder and harder to tell the good from the bad.

It seems there are no longer any criteria by which to judge what is beautiful or worthwhile, but I believe the criteria exist; they are just more difficult to find. I believe the new art must not exclude the old; nor should it simply appropriate the old without any critical discernment. There is still a need for beauty, and I believe there are still good reasons for making informed, qualitative judgments about art. If we simply accept everything willy-nilly, then nothing is of value. The indiscriminate acceptance of anything and everything lessens the value of everything. By way of analogy, how would we ever learn to appreciate the beauty of William Shakespeare's plays if the only theater we were ever exposed to was "Cats" or the complexity of Beethoven if the only music we ever heard was Pat Boone's "Love Letters in the Sand"? Without some means of judging quality in art, much of art would sink to the level of soap operas and romance novels and syrupy love songs. How then do we decide what is good and what is not when the art we see ranges from performance art to piles of dirt to traditional painting and sculpture?

There are no easy answers. I have tried throughout this book to offer some guidelines. For judging painting and sculpture, many of the old criteria still apply — what the critic Clive Bell called significant form, harmony and rhythm, exciting color combinations, variety within unity, interesting textures and lyrical lines. For art whose purpose is more social or political than aesthetic, we may have to look to literature, theater and music for criteria. What is the artist trying to say, and how well did he or she say it? Is the statement profound, original or provocative, or is it trite or silly or clichéd? I believe we must each try to answer these questions in our own way, but we should try to become informed and approach art with an open mind. The old saw "I don't know much about art but I know what I like" just will not do.

www.ingramcontent.com/pod-product-compliance
Lightning Source LLC
LaVergne TN
LVHW020644100826
845148LV00012B/2324

* 9 7 8 0 9 8 0 0 3 2 2 4 6 *